WHAT
AM I
THINKING?

DANNY TICE

ISBN: 0-9817608-8-0
978-0-9817608-8-9

Published by

LIFEBRIDGE
BOOKS
P.O. BOX 49428
CHARLOTTE, NC 28277

Printed in the United States of America.
Author's photo by Theis Photography, Ltd.

DEDICATION

This book is dedicated to my wife, Karen, the one true love of my life.

WHAT THEY SAY

In an "I could have had a V-8!" world, many of us could have had some different thoughts. Pastor Danny Tice, from years of experience as a pastor, counselor, husband, father, and friend, has walked with many people through the "consequences" of poor thinking. He puts his finger on a huge issue in our society: The Misery Distortion Complex. And if "misery wants company," Pastor Tice offers readers a clear alternative.

So, if you have been camping out in "failure land," Pastor Danny offers a roadmap for a way out and a way up. His stories will make you laugh AND they will make you ask: "What am I thinking?" Buy an extra copy or two: someone you know will need this book first thing in the morning.

    – Dr. Harold Ivan Smith, popular speaker and
      educator.

"Danny's new book is just like him—POSITIVE! In these days when everything around the world is about "me," it's high time to hear about "others!" *What Am I Thinking?* enables you to live a life that SERVES and GIVES, which can only be done with a positive life and attitude! But the good thing is this, when you serve and give, YOU are positive! Go figure!

So, get a good cup of coffee...take a seat in your favorite chair and have a great read! You will get a "pick me up"—and it won't be the caffeine!

    – Dr. Dennis "The Swan" Swanberg, America's
      Minister of Encouragement

CONTENTS

1 ATTITUDE IS A CHOICE   7

2 THE DANGER OF "COMPARISON" THINKING   29

3 RECOVERING FROM FAILURE   47

4 ELIMINATING OUR DISTANCE FROM GOD   71

5 WHAT ARE YOU EXPECTING?   89

6 SERVANTHOOD 101   115

7 MENTAL WEARINESS   123

8 THINKING TOO MUCH ABOUT TOMORROW   139

EPILOGUE   154

ACKNOWLEDGMENTS   157

1

ATTITUDE
IS A CHOICE

*You are free the moment you do
not look outside yourself for someone
to solve your problems.*

– ANONYMOUS

The most positive person I know is my wife Karen. She seems to be able to always find the silver lining in any cloud.

The way she approaches life reminds me of the story Ronald Reagan used to illustrate optimism when he was President of the United States. Reagan's story revolved around a young boy who discovered a room full of manure and quipped, "There must be a pony in here somewhere!"

That is optimism at its finest.

Karen has a way of being positive in any situation. By temperament she is more optimistic than I am—I tend to be more critical and pessimistic. Why I am this way is anyone's guess. Is my tendency to be more negative than my wife because of my early environment or my genetics?

The court is still out on the nurture versus nature debate.

The court is still out on the nurture versus nature debate. One thing is for sure: some of us tend to be more negative than others. I believe, however, regardless of how prone we are to negativity, we can train ourselves to see the brighter side of life.

I truly believe we have met the enemy, and it is us.

WHAT STINKS?

Popular motivational speaker Zig Ziglar once told the amusing story of a grandfather who was sleeping. His mischievous grandchildren quietly went to the refrigerator and pulled out the smelly Limburger cheese that was sitting on the shelf of the refrigerator. They carefully smeared some of the cheese onto their grandfather's mustache.

A few minutes later, after the kids had escaped the living room, their grandfather woke up with a perplexed look on his face. Wiggling his nose, he commented, "This living room stinks." He walked out into the kitchen and exclaimed, "Man the kitchen stinks." Then he walked outside and complained, "The whole world stinks!"

Often we blame what is offensive in our life on the environment around us. We attribute the negative way we feel about the world to our circumstances when, in reality, the key to a more positive future is how we manage our attitude.

"THE LAST OF HUMAN FREEDOMS"

Let me share with you the heart-wrenching story of Victor Frankl. Here was a man who knew hardship and suffering personally. He was a psychiatrist and neurologist who had a very successful counseling practice in Vienna, Austria. In the years prior to World War II, Frankl was incarcerated by the Nazis and was shipped to Auschwitz and later moved to Dachau.

During these dark years when the Hitler regime insanely destroyed human life, Frankl witnessed the death of his mother and father, his brother, and finally his beloved pregnant wife at the hands of the Nazis.

Yet, despite the horrific loss of his family, Frankl encouraged his fellow prisoners not to abandon hope and submit to despair or suicide. He wrote his thoughts concerning hope and life on stolen pieces of paper that became a book, *Man's Search for Meaning*. The book sold over ten million copies and was printed in 24 languages after his release from the concentration camps in 1945.

On one of these scraps of paper Frankl wrote, "The last of human freedoms is to choose one's attitude in any given set of circumstances."

Knowing Frankl's personal background makes this

statement profound. It was not written in the context of a peaceful and placid existence, rather as a persecuted Jew exposed to the darkest human experience possible.

Human beings, according to Frankl, have the capacity to create their own attitude. If his statement was true for Frankl in dire circumstances, it can be true for you and me in less challenging environments.

IT'S A CHOICE

The most important ingredient to success is your outlook. A good attitude will take you further in life than money, talent, or good luck. It will also make the journey much more pleasant.

Life's pathway can be gloomy and melancholy or it can be jubilant and joyful. Attitude is an essential commodity for personal happiness.

What we are discussing is not a spiritual gift, rather a discipline. A good attitude is not a temperament, nor a family trait, and certainly not something believers in God automatically possess. It is a choice.

You and I have the capacity to make a choice regarding how we view the world. In a real sense we choose our feelings; our feelings don't choose us.

Of course, there are hormones and brain chemistry that orient our moods in certain directions at times, but too many of us have been guilty of immediately giving in to these raging emotional forces.

DESTRUCTIVE WINDS

We often mistakenly approach life like sailors in a boat. We unfurl our sails to the present prevailing winds. The sails are representative of our human will while the winds correspond to our negative emotions. When a negative life experience overwhelms us, we too quickly embrace the destructive winds of doubt and despair.

To use a sports metaphor, we often allow our thoughts to be booted around like a soccer ball that is kicked in many directions. When our thoughts and emotions regarding how we feel about our current circumstances pull us down unhealthy paths, we need to summon the courage and tenacity necessary to redirect those thoughts and feelings. It is time for us to take responsibility for our attitude in life.

RESPONSIBILITY = EMPOWERMENT

Taking ownership of our thoughts and emotions empowers us. When we believe we have the power to direct our own thoughts and feelings, our discouragement and gloom begin to dissipate.

> *Taking ownership of our thoughts and emotions empowers us.*

Most depressed people think they are powerless to rule over their negative feelings. They believe they are hostage to the dark clouds in their soul. Sadly, many conclude that their current emotional state is their destiny and they can do very little about it.

Unfortunately our beliefs become our reality. A proverb from the pen of King Solomon underscores this truth: *"For as he [a man] thinketh in his heart, so is he"* (Proverbs 23:7 KJV).

Taking command of our feelings is often difficult to do but, in most cases, unless there is a severe emotional disorder, we *can* do something regarding our attitude and emotional state. The moment we begin to realize we are not victims we are on the road to victory. This paradigm shift regarding how we view life gives us foothold to move on to a more positive tomorrow.

The moment we begin to realize we are not victims we are on the road to victory.

Empowerment elevates while dis-empowerment destroys hope and shrouds one's emotions in gloom and doom.

RISING ABOVE VICTIM MENTALITY

I have friends who are counselors. Many of them do a terrific job helping people. They tell me that their clients need to leave a counseling session feeling empowered—knowing that they can contribute to their own personal progress toward a more positive future. Any counseling that does not challenge individuals to play an active role in their attitude elevation is not the right kind of guidance.

Counselors need to be empathetic and loving, but

their clients must be challenged to rise above the victim mentality and take an active part in embracing responsibility altering their emotions and attitude. Any counseling that makes an individual view him or herself as a total victim is ultimately not helpful.

Stephen Covey, in his book *Seven Habits of Effective People,* says this about our personal responsibility for the state of our lives:

> *Look at the word responsibility— "response- ability'"— the ability to choose your response. Highly proactive people recognize that responsi- bility. They do not blame circumstance, condi- tions, or conditioning for their behavior. Their behavior is the product of their own conscious choice, based on values, rather than a product of their conditions, based on feeling.*

Covey's insight is that we have the ability to choose our response to any given situation. I can, and you can, respond to where we are in a positive and healthy way.

DEPRESSION AND MEDICATION

Some individuals experience serious depression and struggle with severe melancholy. There are times when such dark moods are a result of deficient serotonin in our brains. No Christian should ever feel guilty about taking medication for depression if it is necessary. God has

13

made us body, soul, and spirit; yet sometimes our bodies need extra help in balancing natural chemical deficiencies.

However, while medication is needed on occasion for deficient levels of serotonin in our brain, there is no substitute for our proactive involvement in our own personal well-being. Any doctor or counselor who slides a pill across the table and claims, "This pill will solve all of your emotional problems," is misleading his or her clients.

One of the ways I personally alleviate melancholy feelings and sadness is to jump on the treadmill for a half hour of invigorating exercise. The oxygen going to my brain increases the dopamine it needs and my emotional state is improved, not to mention my heart.

WHOSE FAULT?

Someone once said, "Our bodies and souls are close neighbors." What happens to one affects the other. If I exercise my body, my soul, which is where my emotions reside, will benefit as well. Every human being has been impacted by life's experiences. Our parents, plus our environment, leave their mark on us, but those imprints cannot be our excuse to be perpetually encased in gloom and despair. This modern

> *If I exercise my body, my soul, which is where my emotions reside, will benefit as well.*

folk song by Anna Russell cleverly outlines a prevalent attitude of many individuals:

I went to my psychiatrist to be psychoanalyzed,
To find out why I killed the cat and blacked my
husband's eyes.
He laid me on a downy couch to see what he
could find,
And here is what he dredged up from my
subconscious mind:
When I was one, my mommie hid my dolly in a
trunk,
And so it follows naturally that I am always
drunk.
When I was two, I saw my father kiss the maid
one day,
And that is why I suffer from kleptomania.
At three, I had the feeling of ambivalence toward
my brothers,
And so it follows naturally I poison all my lovers.
But I am so happy; now I've learned the lesson
this has taught;
That everything I do that's wrong is someone
else's fault.

ESCAPING THE PRISON OF DESPAIR

Owning our emotions and thoughts is imperative before we can move forward in life. We must personally "look out for our outlook."

The minute we fall prey to the idea that we have no "response-ability" we begin to view ourselves as victims overpowered by a life whose emotional fate is sealed. This perspective of lack of empowerment will breed hopelessness in our heart and we will be locked in the prison of despair.

In pastoral counseling over the years I have noticed that as soon as people are challenged to be accountable for their attitude and feelings, they begin to improve emotionally. The "powerlessness paradigm" insists that we are incapable of changing where we are in life emotionally. "I am trapped," we say to ourselves. No wonder people are depressed if they believe they are hopelessly entangled in the circumstances in which they find themselves.

MOSES' CRY OF POWERLESSNESS

One of my favorite stories in the Bible is the commissioning of Moses to go to Egypt to lead the children of Israel out of bondage. These famous relatives of Moses had been captive in Egypt for 400 years. (See Genesis 13:13; Acts 7:6.)

Moses had made an attempt, forty years earlier, to rescue some of his people from their bondage of oppression but had miserably failed. Now, four decades later, God arrives on the scene in the form of a burning bush to commission him anew to liberate the Israelites from their burdened station in life.

The now eighty-year-old Moses offers God a litany of excuses for why he is unable to help the suffering of his people. Moses asks, *"Who am I, that I should go to Pharaoh and bring the Israelites out of Egypt?"* (Exodus 3:11).

He is arguing that he is insignificant and does not have what it takes to alleviate the condition of the Israelites. Moses is saying to the Lord, "I am only a shepherd. I do not have the political clout to challenge Pharaoh."

Such reasoning leaves Moses powerless. He is having a confidence crisis and sees himself as inept in the face of the current challenge. Moses' focus was in *his* *insufficiency*, not in God's amazing *sufficiency*.

"I WILL HELP YOU"

When belief in our own incompetence settles upon us, we are already defeated. Despair is always close on the heels of an attitude of powerlessness.

There must be a major shift in our thinking. Our confidence crisis must be crushed and replaced with new faith and trust in God's willingness to partner

❖

When belief in our own incompetence settles upon us, we are already defeated.

with us to pull ourselves and others out of the pit of defeat and despair.

17

God's rebuttal to Moses is simple: *"And God said, 'I will be with you. And this will be the sign to you that it is I who have sent you: When you have brought the people out of Egypt, you will worship God on this mountain'"* (Exodus 3:12).

The lesson in God's response is clear. The massive changes that have to be made for a more positive future do not have to be made alone.

"I will help you, Moses," says the Lord. In other words, without God he would fail, but with Him he would succeed. The changes which must be achieved *can* be made with the help of our heavenly Father.

A "CAN DO" SPIRIT

The Apostle Paul weighs in on this point when he writes, *"I can do everything through him who gives me strength" (Philippians 4:13).*

Paul wrote these words from a prison in Rome. He was not a guest at the Hyatt Regency, resting comfortably on a king-size bed. His circumstances, not unlike Victor Frankl's, were less than perfect. He had challenges but he did not allow them to darken his attitude. Paul exhibited a "can-do" spirit that was birthed out of his partnership with the Lord. It kept him full of joy and he was extremely productive during this stage of his life. His attitude was bright in spite of less than ideal circumstances.

Our journey toward success is not a solo one, but is

accomplished in tandem with the Lord's help. We must always do our part and keep moving forward toward the vision God has for us.

The words of Jesus bring hope to those of us who have experienced struggle and despair. His words ring throughout generations; they are familiar yet profound. You have heard them from your childhood:, *"Come to me, all you who are weary and burdened, and I will give you rest. Take my yoke upon you and learn from me, for I am gentle and humble in heart, and you will find rest for your souls. For my yoke is easy and my burden is light"* (Matthew 11:28-30).

> There are still fields to be plowed, but there is a divine partner with you in every aspect of your journey.

The picture painted by Jesus here is one of draft (working) animals that were used in ancient Israel to plow the fields of Palestine. Two animals yoked at the neck working side by side pulling a plow were able to easily handle the weight tethered to them.

Jesus is giving an alternative to facing life alone without His help. It is hard when you try to handle stress all by yourself, but when you are yoked with Jesus, your days are much easier. The challenges are still present. There are still fields to be plowed, but there is a divine partner with you in every aspect of your journey.

A DIVINE NETWORK

Recently my son Tim was married. He and his

beautiful bride, Gillie, were wed on the sea shore near Rehoboth Beach, Delaware, at 10 A.M. on a lovely September Saturday morning.

After the ceremony everyone rushed to our church for the reception—a brunch with an omelet bar, pancakes, and all the delicious breakfast foods you could imagine.

After the dancing and fun were over they departed in their car to head off for their honeymoon. Soon afterward the well-fed guests also left for a leisurely weekend.

Our church sanctuary is a multi-purpose room that is used for banquets, basketball games, and worship services. Because the wedding reception had transformed the sanctuary into a banquet room, with round tables and food stations, everything had to be disassembled and reset. Hundreds of chairs had to be rearranged to accommodate our congregation for the regular weekend services.

This task was manageable because the undertaking was not tackled alone.

The two days prior to the wedding had been exhausting with many last minute details to finalize. Now the hours of set up time were before us. Thankfully I had asked some of my closest friends ahead of time if they would stay to assist Karen and me in this Herculean task.

Without any hesitation my friends and their wives stood shoulder to shoulder with us as we arranged hundreds of chairs. The task was manageable because the undertaking was not tackled alone.

Likewise, we can handle the countless challenges we face during our lifetime if we have created a circle of support. That divine network is our relationship with the Lord Himself and with His people.

GUARDING YOUR MIND

Each morning I begin my day with prayer, and during those early morning hours I ask the Lord to give me His grace and strength for the many issues I am facing and currently dealing with. In some cases, I have unique wisdom from the Lord imparted to me; at other times I have no idea how I am going to be able to deal with the problems.

However, after committing my needs to the Lord, I have a new sense of inner peace.

In the New Testament the apostle Paul wrote a short letter to a group of Christian believers in the town of Philippi. His writing from prison gives candid advice on how to relieve stress in life. He counsels: *"Do not be anxious about anything, but in everything, by prayer and petition, with thanksgiving, present your request to God. And the peace of God, which transcends all understanding, will guard your heart and your minds in Christ Jesus"* (Philippians 4:6-7).

Unlike Paul, Moses—in the early stages of his conversation with God on the side of the mountain—had not yet achieved the peace and confidence of the Lord. Thankfully, the Almighty was not yet finished speaking to Moses. He challenged this future leader to recognize that he was not weak and powerless, but had the potential and the strength, with God's help, to do something about the current state of affairs he and the children of Israel were in.

THE GREAT "I AM"

As the Exodus 3 story unfolds, Moses continues to argue with God regarding his powerlessness to do anything about the negative experiences of the people in Egypt. His excuses were as long as the Nile River. He was concerned that he did not know how to articulate who God truly is.

Moses questions, "I don't even know your name" (my paraphrase). God's response is legendary: "*I am who I am. This is what you are to say to the Israelites: 'I AM has sent me to you'*" (Exodus 3:14).

What does this phrase, "I am who I am" really mean? It simply is a statement of being. God is letting Moses know, "I exist. My being is a reality and if I am real, then that revolutionary realization should forever change your outlook."

Unfortunately many times we are lost and flounder through life as if God is not a reality. We live as if the great "I am" is the great "I am not."

IS GOD DEAD?

Martin Luther, the renowned Protestant reformer, was

under enormous pressure from the Pope for his supposed heretical beliefs. At one point Luther became very discouraged, and this turned into depression. He sat in a state of melancholy in his house for days on end, feeling sorry for himself and filled with despair.

After watching this drama of grief unfold, his wife did something to try and snap him out of his negative self-made prison. Luther's wife came down the stairs wearing a black dress accessorized with a black veil covering her face. Luther looked at her and asked, "Where are you going dressed like that?"

"I am going to a funeral," she quipped.

"Whose funeral?" he wanted to know.

"Where are you going dressed like that?"

"I am going to God's funeral because you are living as if He has died!" she responded.

There are times we live this way, too. However, the fact is that God is not dead; He is very much alive. His existence and providential care for His children should catapult us into a different mindset. Our misery doesn't have to rule over us because "I am that I am" is always present.

USE WHAT YOU HAVE

In the story of Moses, God finally asks, *"What is that in your hand?"* (Exodus 4:2).

Moses was holding the staff that God would use to liberate His people from their oppressed state in Egypt. This word from God came to Moses in the context of darkness and suffering. The people were crushed and depressed, and Moses felt hopeless in his belief that nothing could be done to remedy their situation.

God, however, refused to let Moses plead incompetence. His alibis were not working on the Lord. "Moses, you have something right in your hand that you can use to turn around the situation. You are not powerless; you have a rod that has incredible potential."

The Lord was telling Moses, "Take what you have in your hand and change your future. Stop being a victim and take action regarding the plight of you and your people by using what you can control."

Moses did not have authority over Pharaoh or the Egyptian nation—or the circumstances that swirled around the Israelites in this season of their history. But there was something he *could* do. He could control the staff in his hand.

There are many aspects of life we cannot take charge of, but we can control our attitude—and how we choose to view our lives with the blend of good and bad that we all experience.

When Moses did what he *could* do, God stepped in and did what Moses *couldn't* do.

The lesson is clear. When we take charge of our renegade thoughts and feelings, God begins to perform amazing miracles in our lives.

TAKE CHARGE OF YOUR THOUGHTS

The Bible lets us know it is possible to manage and control our thought life. If this were not the case, why would God have challenged us to redirect our pessimistic thinking? We learn this truth again from the Apostle Paul as he wrote from prison in Rome: *"Finally, brothers, whatever is true, whatever is noble, whatever is right, whatever is pure, whatever is lovely, whatever is admirable—if anything is excellent or praiseworthy—think about such things"* (Philippians 4:8).

❖

We have the power to choose what we dwell on.

Paul's last phrase is instructive: "think about such things." This means we have the power to choose what we dwell on. Our thoughts affect our feelings, and therefore we can control our emotional well-being by how we choose to think.

"GET OUT OF MY CAR!"

Let me tell you about an elderly woman who came out from the grocery store with her arms filled with grocery bags. When she arrived at her car she saw four white males seated inside. She calmly put down the groceries, pulled a hand gun out of her purse, and walked to the driver's side of the car.

Raising the weapon, she demanded, "Get out of my car right now; I have a gun, and I'm not afraid to use it."

Four frightened men dove out of the vehicle and ran across the grocery store parking lot. The woman then loaded her groceries into the back seat of the car and proceeded to sit in the driver's seat and insert the key into the ignition. The key wouldn't fit!

It was at this point she realized she was in the wrong car. Her vehicle, identical to the one she was now sitting in, was four parking spaces down. She moved her groceries into her own car and proceeded to drive to the police station.

When she arrived and approached the counter to report what she had mistakenly done, the police sergeant listening to her story doubled over in laughter. He pointed down the counter to four shaken white men who had just reported a car theft by a mad and wild elderly woman!

This story lets us know how important it is to eject any negative thinking from our minds. If we allow dark and negative images to remain constantly in our minds, we need to be vigilant and on the alert to rid ourselves of such destructive thinking.

As believers, we each have a spiritual weapon—in the form of Scripture and the Lord's promises to us. We have a God-given mandate to expel negative thinking and replace it with thoughts that are honorable to Him.

It's Your Move

Years ago I heard a message preached in which the

minister described a painting that was hanging in a certain art gallery. The picture portrayed the devil playing chess with Faust (the German medieval scholar who made a pact with the devil).

Depicted in the painting, the devil has a morbid and gleeful grin on his face as he looks at the scholar, but Faust wears a look of hopelessness because he believes himself to be checkmated by the devil.

Year after year people poured through the museum viewing the depressive work of art. Many stood there examining the image on the canvas and identified with Faust and his hopeless plight. Some felt trapped and stuck in life just like this man.

The visitors to the art museum related to Faust's predicament.

One day a chess master was touring the museum and came upon the famous painting. He stood for hours examining the remaining chess pieces on the board featured in the painting. All at once he shouted, "It's a lie! The rook and the bishop still have moves; Faust isn't in checkmate."

The chess master saw moves and possibilities no one else had seen before.

My friend, you still have moves available, and you are not powerless. With God's help, your attitude of hope will elevate your spirit, so you can move forward and enjoy the kind of life you have always dreamed of living.

2

THE DANGER OF "COMPARISON" THINKING

Comparisons breed insecurity, yet we commonly make them among our children, co-workers, and other acquaintances.

— STEPHEN COVEY

When I was a teenager we had a youth choir in my dad's church that was directed by my future sister-in-law, Vicky Moore.

Vicky was successful in recruiting between 30 and 50 high school students for a teen church choir. With her musical knowledge and motivational gifts she was able to weld together a phenomenal group.

The raw adolescent material she was working with was unskilled in four-part harmony. The boys, with their ever-changing voices, attempted to sing tenor and bass, while the young ladies sang alto and soprano. As Vicky tried to find musical arrangements that would facilitate young vocalists, she happened upon the old Negro spiritual, *"Nobody Knows the Trouble I've Seen; Nobody Knows But Jesus."*

This colonial classic had deep and meaningful lyrics and a simple musical score that could easily be performed by novices when it came to four part harmony.

How ironic it was that teenagers with few real troubles in this world would sing a song written by African slaves that knew first hand the depths of emotional and physical suffering.

The most significant trial we as teens were facing was the emergence of fresh pimples that were assaulting our complexion for a few days or not being able to obtain a date for the homecoming dance on Friday evening.

Our troubles were minuscule in comparison to the Negro slaves who birthed these lyrics out of genuine oppression and pain.

THERE'S NO MAGIC WAND

The words of this classic song often reflect our internal mantra as modern Americans. We believe our personal troubles are unique and more significant than the challenges which other people face. This is neither accurate nor is it a healthy viewpoint.

The truth is that all of us are visited by problems sometime in our lives. Like the Old Testament figure named Job, each of us have seasons of trials and pain. Notice how Job summarizes the fact of universal human struggles in his writings: *"Yet man is born unto trouble, as the sparks fly upward"* (Job 32:9).

Job's words are universally true; trouble is not unique to just our lives but is common to all men. Looks can be deceiving. Just because others appear to be happy and carefree doesn't mean they avoid deep valleys.

❖

Just because others appear to be happy and carefree doesn't mean they avoid deep valleys.

We often lack knowledge concerning the real adversity status of our neighbors and co-workers. We do not know what battles they are currently facing, but our ignorance in no way lessens the fact that these men and women may be enduring a crisis, be it small or great.

We are in this thing called life together and all have painful issues to deal with. If there were a magic wand that could instantly eliminate our personal challenges, we would all certainly utilize it.

THE MISERY DISTORTION COMPLEX

One of the biggest hindrances in having a positive attitude is what I call the *misery distortion complex*. This is a life perspective that says, "I have problems, but other people do not. Adversity has signaled me out of the crowd."

31

The *misery distortion complex* views people from a surface level and comes up with the false conclusion that their life is all good while mine is mostly bad.

I once saw a children's cartoon on television that featured a little bald-headed man walking along a road. There was a cloud hovering above his head that followed him wherever he went—and poured rain and thunder down upon his bald head.

The cloud was the exact width of his body, and the rain fell only on him, while all around the people were experiencing sunshine and clear skies. He alone was the recipient of the downpour.

Countless people feel this way, but the image the cartoon portrays is clearly false. We are not the only individuals that encounter stormy days or rainy seasons in our lives. Everyone does.

WHO HAS IT TOUGHER?

Men and women who believe they alone are the recipients of bad things are captive to the *misery distortion complex*. They falsely are of the opinion their days are darker and more challenging than that of the average person. For example, some husbands believe their life situation is more burdensome than their wife's. From the male perspective, he works much harder. He has to get up earlier and go to work each day while she stays home with the four children, all of whom are under five years of age.

"What does she do with all her time?" he muses to himself. "Day after day I have to go out and earn the bacon (the money); the financial pressure rests entirely on my shoulders. She, on the other hand, shuffles around playing with the kids in her fuzzy bedroom slippers and her egg-stained robe as I leave for work."

"What does she do with all her time?"

On the other side of the coin, his wife thinks to herself, "Wow! He has it made. He can escape this zoo (our loving home) every morning and venture into the real world and have a real life and talk to real people who can string full sentences together."

She personally laments the fact it is her total responsibility to change diapers and feed drooling kids while "wonderful daddy" gets to dress up and interact with civilization.

Each of the respective spouses views his or her role as more challenging than the other's. Both of them believe that their world is more difficult than that of their marriage partner.

Often, singles tend to view the married with envy while the married on occasion look on single people with a twinge of jealousy. Each conclude they have it harder.

Someone once observed, "If envy were an illness, the world would be a hospital."

IS THE GRASS REALLY GREENER?

This common distortion is not limited to the sphere of

marriage and singleness. It can occur in other contexts as well. In the arena of vocations, for example:

- Management thinks it has it harder than labor—and vice versa.
- Plumbers think they have it harder than electricians—and vice versa.
- White-collar workers think they have it harder than blue-collar workers—and vice versa.

Stressed out doctors wish they had an easier occupation with more leisure time on their hands and less paperwork, while the taxicab driver wishes he had gone to medical school to become a doctor.

Everyone believes his career and field of work is more stressful than his neighbor's.

Everyone believes his career and field of work is more stressful than his neighbor's. But in reality, each station in life involves responsibility and sacrifice.

Christian counselor and radio host James Dobson once wisely quipped, "The grass may be greener on the other side but it still needs to be mowed."

"WHATEVER" THE CIRCUMSTANCES

The disease of discontentment is rampant—and it is birthed out of the unwise habit of comparison.

It is always unwise to measure our station in life with

that of other people. We each need to arrive at the place reached by the apostle Paul, who said, *"I have learned to be content whatever the circumstances"* (Philippians 4:11). Remember, Paul wrote this while he was confined in prison.

Contentment is not a matter of where we are physically, geographically, or in terms of our circumstances. What counts is where we are in our thoughts and attitude.

THE CONFESSION OF A
DISCOURAGED MUSICIAN

The Bible features a man who had a serious "misery distortion complex." His name was Asaph, and he was a musician and worship leader in the ancient temple of the Israelites. The *Archeological Bible* says this about Asaph:

> *Unlike David, who was a renowned and yet amateur musician, Asaph, Heman, Ethan and the sons of Korah were in effect professional singers who created and sang psalms as part of their Levitical service in the temple. Asaph, a Levitical choir leader during the time of David (1 Chronicles 6:39), is mentioned along side David in 2 Chronicles 29:30 as a composer of psalms and as "seer." He is credited with Psalms 50 and 73-83.*

Asaph held a grand spiritual position in the ancient world of ministry. He was a man who wrote songs (psalms) and heard the Lord speak to him in powerful ways. He also was a companion and co-minister of King David.

Despite all of these positives in his life, he still struggled emotionally. Asaph's difficulties were in the arena of comparing his lot in life with those around him. In fact, their lives looked far more appealing than his own!

The problem was not that Asaph wasn't a spiritual person; he was. Spiritual individuals are not exempt from possessing a skewed perspective. In fact, a distorted viewpoint can plague a Christian just as easily as it can a non-believer.

PLAGUED AND PUNISHED?

Listen to the words of Asaph as he laments over his circumstances. His melancholy message has much to teach us concerning guarding our hearts from a bad attitude when we begin to compare ourselves to others:

Surely God is good to Israel, to those who are pure in heart. But as for me, my feet had almost slipped; I had nearly lost my foothold. For I envied the arrogant when I saw the prosperity of the wicked. They have no struggles; their bodies are healthy and strong. They are free from the

36

burdens common to man; they are not plagued by human ills.

This is what the wicked are like—always carefree, they increase in wealth. Surely in vain have I kept my heart pure; in vain have I washed my hands in innocence. All day long I have been plagued; I have been punished every morning (Psalm 73:1-5, 12-14).

Asaph's emotional distortion is common to many of us from time to time. He bemoans the wicked who prosper and seem to have no problems; that they are healthy, strong and free from what besets most people.

Is this accurate? Do others, particularly unbelievers, escape struggles?

❖

When our heart is burdened with troubles it manufactures a false reality.

Asaph is dejected—and downhearted people do not see things accurately. In short, discouragement causes our perspective to be distorted. When our heart is burdened with troubles it manufactures a false reality.

We know that Asaph is overwhelmed by what he writes in verse 14: "All day long I have been plagued; I have been punished every morning."

THE WRONG VIEW

Never trust your judgement when you are downcast.

This is when small problems seem huge, and your dreams are dashed.

The inaccuracies in Asaph's words are clear. According to his assessment, the wicked are exempt from any kind of trouble or woe. They seem to have a free pass when it comes to adversity. Asaph-type individuals see others this way: "Their life is awesome while mine is awful. They never get sick, they never stub their toe, and their children always behave."

Playing the comparison game is dangerous because it only contributes to our negativity and pessimism.

This is the negative viewpoint we tend to adopt when we are disheartened. This man, who saw the wicked as carefree and increasing in riches, teaches us a powerful lesson. Playing the comparison game is dangerous because it only contributes to our negativity and pessimism.

I have observed that when we measure our lives against our neighbor's, we chose individuals who we think have it better than we do—not with those who are less fortunate.

HARDSHIP IS RELATIVE

Recently I helped with a feeding program sponsored by a ministry in our church. This outreach regularly goes to an area in a nearby city where many are homeless. The ministry provides warm soup, sandwiches, cookies, and water or sodas for the homeless to enjoy.

As I stood there greeting these thankful people as they received our assistance, I realized that my challenges were insignificant compared to theirs. The struggle to obtain the most basic daily necessities was their constant plight.

Hardship indeed is relative. Dynamic author and communicator Charles Simpson from Mobile, Alabama, tells this humorous story in his book, *Son Take your Hat Off*:

> *Many years ago there was a man who survived the Jonestown flood—a very famous, devastating flood. Many times he was asked to give his testimony on how he survived. Finally, the man passed on and went to heaven where no one called on him to testify about it. Finally, he asked if he could give his testimony since he had done that so many times when he was down on the earth, and he thought everyone might be interested. They gave him a spot on the program —right after Noah.*

Mature people are able to recalculate their tendency toward self-pity and realize that there are always others who have experienced a more damaging storm than they have.

WHEN WE ARE GOING THROUGH A SIGNIFICANT TRIAL

Unfortunately, at some point, pain is everybody's portion. However, life is not one long trial; our lives are often interspersed with great joy and many pleasant days. Let's compare this to the world of weather. Every year there is a hurricane season, but it doesn't last forever. This is also true of adversity and trouble. We can take comfort in the words of the old country preacher who said his favorite verse in the Bible was: "And it came to pass."

Thankfully, trials do have a termination date. Despite the *misery distortion complex*, the truth is that there are seasons in which some suffer more than others. But this doesn't alter the fact the intensity of trials is not equally distributed—any more than the temperature across each region in the country is the same.

Florida is bathed in sunshine at the exact same time Maine is fighting a major blizzard. Although it is conversely true that sometimes the hurricane winds are clobbering Florida while Maine experiences a calm gentle breeze. This is also the case for us as certain individuals endure a horrendous season of life while others are enjoying relative calm. Perhaps because of a sickness, wayward children, trouble in business or finances, a miscarriage, or some betrayal by a dear friend, their world is currently a dismal swamp.

If there were such a thing as a "trouble scale," certain

individuals would tip the balance far more than others.

GRACE AND STRENGTH

We should always remember that when we are battling a dreadful season, God has sufficient grace for us—and His divine strength is proportional to where we are on our life's journey.

This was the lesson Paul taught us in his candid second letter to the Corinthians. No other writings of the apostle rival his honesty concerning his personal

> *His divine strength is proportional to where we are on our life's journey.*

feelings than this letter. He is brutally honest and confesses about his mysterious thorn in the flesh:

> *To keep me from becoming conceited because of these surpassingly great revelations, there was given me a thorn in my flesh, a messenger of Satan, to torment me. Three times I pleaded with the Lord to take it away from me. But he said to me, "My grace is sufficient for you, for my power is made perfect in weakness." Therefore I will boast all the more gladly about my weaknesses, so that Christ's power may rest on me* (2 Corinthians 12:7-9).

Paul's prayer was not answered the way he wished. He wanted the painful affliction to automatically go away.

41

Many have conjectured what Paul's thorn was: an eye disease, malaria, trouble from persecutors, or even an unhappy marriage.

The true identity of the thorn is unimportant. The fact remains, Paul had something in his life that troubled him; he wanted it gone but God allowed it to remain. Paul longed for the Lord to adjust his circumstances, but God chose instead to strengthen his heart and give him divine resolve: "My grace and My strength are sufficient for you."

GOD'S "MATCHING GRACE" PROGRAM

Thankfully, the level of trial we face is accompanied by the same level of strength that comes from the Lord. If we are up against a mountain that is unprecedented, the needed amount of divine power will be available. Let me illustrate this in terms of measurements of weight:

- If we have a 10-pound trial we receive 10 pounds of strength from the Lord.
- If we have a 50-pound trial we receive 50 pounds of strength from the Lord.
- If we have a 1000-pound trial we receive 1000 pounds of strength from the Lord.

We realize this principle when we look back with amazement on the troublesome seasons of our past. "How did I get through that rough patch?" we exclaim.

"I don't know how I did it," we say to ourselves.

We finally realize we had enough resolve because of God's amazing "matching grace" program. He gives us His special grace when we are enduring a uniquely challenging time.

The good news about this reality is that when we face future adversity, the Lord's grace will be increased in proportion to the trial we encounter. This explains Paul's famous statement:

> *He gives us His special grace when we are enduring a uniquely challenging time.*

"I can do all things through him that strengthens me" (Philippians 4:13)

This is not a verse about winning the slam-dunk contests hosted by ESPN. Paul wrote these words behind prison bars. It was an exceptionally difficult time for him, but he received the strength from the Lord at that point in his life.

HE CAN CARRY YOU SAFELY TO THE OTHER SIDE

I love the account of Charles Blondin the French acrobat who performed in the United States in the early 1900s. Blondin was most famous for his high wire acts above Niagara Falls.

A tight wire was stretched across the famous falls, and Blondin amazed the crowds with his daring feats over the dangerous waters. His connection with the onlookers at these performances was legendary.

Often he would taunt those watching with his antics. He would hold up a chair and say, "Who believes I can carry this chair across to the other side and back?"

The crowd, wild with excitement, would reply, "You can do it Charles! You can do anything."

Across the falls he would go, carefully balancing the chair as he made his dangerous trek across the wire.

Returning to the other side he would hold up a small table and ask, "Who believes I am capable of carrying this table across to the other side and back?"

The crowd would be worked into a frenzy. "You can do it Charles, you can do it!"

Across the falls and back he would go, carefully holding the table while traversing the dangerous distance. Finally he would take a wheelbarrow and say to the crowd, "Who believes I can push this wheelbarrow across to the other side and back?"

The crowd would shout in unison, "You can Charles, you can do anything!"

Over and back Charles would go pushing the wheelbarrow.

After returning with the wheelbarrow, he would ask the ultimate question: "Who believes I can push one of you over to the other side in the wheelbarrow?"

Silence enveloped the crowd. No one dared to make eye contact with Charles Blondin because they were unwilling to climb in the wheelbarrow and trust him to ferry them safely to the other side.

WHO DO YOU TRUST?

Most people readily admit they believe God can do anything. But do we trust Him enough to carry us safely through the difficult time we are currently facing?

The answer is an unqualified, "Yes!" Almighty God can be trusted to carry you and me securely through any adversity. Keep your eyes and thoughts firmly fixed on Him instead of comparing your position in life with that of others.

Today, bury "comparison" thinking. After all, you do not receive grace from God to live someone else's life— you have His grace to live *your* life.

3

RECOVERING FROM FAILURE

Success is never final, failure is never fatal.
It is the courage to continue which counts.

– WINSTON CHURCHILL

I made a big mistake when I was about 14 years old. One that, at the time, I feared would have serious consequences. Being 14, I was in the pre-driving stage of my youth. I had, however, a huge desire to drive and couldn't imagine waiting two more years to be behind the wheel of an automobile.

When my parents would leave the house for a brief trip to town or to run an errand, I had the dangerous habit of grabbing the keys to their second car and driving it up and down the driveway beside our house.

Our neighbors must have thought it was quite strange to see the car going forward and backwards over and over again. But the desire to drive coupled with the thrill and danger of fooling my parents had made this renegade habit addictive.

One summer day my parents had gone somewhere and left their large green Chevrolet Impala station wagon (which for our younger readers was an antique mini-van) parked under a maple tree near the house. I seized the keys to this beast of a car, which seemed several blocks long and weighed as much as a small aircraft carrier!

I began my ritual of driving the car up and down the driveway. However, fearing my time of adventure might be running out and that my parents' return was imminent, I approached the maple tree to leave the car precisely where it had been parked.

Unfortunately, as I slowed down and attempted to hit the brakes, I inadvertently hit the gas pedal instead. The huge green Chevrolet Impala crashed into the corner of the house. Shingles flew everywhere!

FRIGHTENED BEYOND WORDS

My heart was pounding and my hands shaking as my brief life passed before my eyes. I was convinced that my parents were going to kill me when they returned home and witnessed the disaster I had caused.

Being raised in a Christian home I immediately thought of the scripture *"...be sure your sin will find you out"* (Numbers 32:23).

I tried to repair the corner of the house before my

parents could see it, but my rudimentary carpentry skills were no match for the damage I had inflicted on our home.

Much to my relief, when my parents learned what had happened, they were so grateful I was not injured that they felt no punishment was necessary. They knew my suffering had been intense waiting for them to return—and that was enough.

LEARN TO "LET GO"

Running the car into your own house qualifies you for the moron of the year award! But in truth, we have all crashed at some point or another due to the poor decisions we have made.

> *It is impossible to have a good outlook on life until we learn to "let go" of our gargantuan goofs.*

It is impossible to have a good outlook on life until we learn to "let go" of our gargantuan goofs.

Let's face it. Mistakes can be paralyzing, but we cannot achieve our potential until we successfully bury them and move on.

Even great leaders make errors, and the most brilliant minds can have a lapse in judgment.

HIDING FROM THE KING

There was a young emerging leader in ancient Israel, some 3000 years ago who made a huge blunder. I'm referring to David, who eventually overcame his transgressions to become Israel's greatest king.

When David was in his youth, he was drafted into King Saul's service. The current King of Israel had some serious insecurity problems and was jealous of David's popularity. Consequently he began to persecute David.

The net result of this harassment led David to become a fugitive, hiding in the woods and caves in Israel.

David had a number of opportunities to kill his nemesis, King Saul, but he wisely refused to harm the man who was causing him such misery. His restraint may have been the awareness that should he kill Saul, he would tragically set in motion a pattern that could bring about his demise when he eventually would ascend to the throne. However, he was weary of the whole process of looking over his shoulder and hiding.

He surmised that one day Saul would eventually capture and kill him (See 1 Samuel 27:1), a situation David was anxious to avoid.

He decided to hide out in the land of Israel's chief antagonist, the Philistines. This strategy revolved around the fact that the Philistines would accept David because they were aware of his troubled relationship with Saul.

COVERT ACTIVITY

David found refuge in one particular Philistine province called Gath, ruled by King Achish. All was well —David and Achish meshed in spirit and purpose, and he thought his problems were solved.

Achish was so grateful for his partnership with David that he gave him a small city to reside in with his wives, his men, and their families. The little town on the edge of the desert was called Ziklag.

During the daytime, using Ziklag as a launching area, David and his 600 hundred member army would conduct covert raids on the surrounding territories. The areas they were systematically obliterating were friendly to the Philistines.

> ❖
>
> *David and his men were secretly whittling away the support base of the Philistine's military alliance.*

In the process, David and his men were secretly whittling away the support base of the Philistine's military alliance. This covert activity continued to help the Israelites.

A SELF-MADE PREDICAMENT

You would think that David wouldn't care about Saul and his people who had made his life so miserable, but David had found a way to still help his beloved nation.

All was well until one day Achish instructed David that he and his men were to join a large Philistine military expedition to go into the land of Israel to fight against King Saul.

How could David do this? It would not only be unethical for him to wage war against his own people, but it would also be a violation of his principle not to touch King Saul, *"the Lord's anointed"* (1 Samuel 24:6).

David probably whispered a prayer under his breath and hoped God would get him out of his self-made predicament. Being a gifted dramatist, David pretended to be supportive and excited about the expedition.

God had mercy on David in this awkward situation and this is how his dilemma was resolved. When the rest of the Philistine leaders saw David and his men, *"these Hebrews"* (1 Samuel 29:3), they protested and convinced Achish to send them back. "How can we trust these Hebrews to go fight Hebrews?" the Philistine commanders wondered.

Consequently, David and his band of soldiers spent the night with the Philistine army, and the next morning began making their way back to Ziklag. The walk took approximately three days.

No doubt their journey was relaxed and leisurely in the wake of having been spared from going to war against their own nation. When they finally reached the outskirts of Ziklag, they could see smoke rising into the sky. The city lay in ashes!

❖

Something terrible had gone wrong.

A CRAZY SCHEME

Something terrible had gone wrong. In the absence of David and his men the bitter Amalekites had invaded

52

Ziklag. He had unwisely left his family and the families of his men unprotected and vulnerable.

David and his men were devastated. As the sorrow and frustration mounted, his warriors began to direct their blame on him. After all, it was David's crazy scheme to come to the Philistine territory in the first place. He had led his men away from the city in the pretense of supporting Achish, but Ziklag had been left completely defenseless because of David's poor judgment. There was no one else to blame.

The accusation against David was well deserved. He had not prayed about coming to the Philistine territory to hide out. Often David asked God for guidance regarding what to do in his journeys, but in this case he had decided to "wing it."

The consequences were now at hand. David's lack of prayer and his huge misjudgment had led to the calamity everyone was now experiencing. His foolish decisions had indeed impacted many people, and his own personal sorrow was compounded by the fact that his men hated him and wished to kill him—not a very strong vote of confidence.

UNLOCKING THE CAGE

However, there is a twist in the story. David's grief was temporary and he began to get a grip on the situation. The Bible tells us, *"But David found strength in the Lord"* (1 Samuel 30:6).

When it would have been so easy for David to wallow in self-pity and regret, he found a way to assert himself. David did not lock himself in the cage of regret; he broke out and moved forward. He called for the priest and received guidance. Then he pursued the Amalekites and recovered what had been stolen.

This nadir moment in David's life teaches us an incredible attitude principle; sustained regret has no workable purpose to improve our lives. If we are going to develop a good attitude, we must rid ourselves of useless regret and move ahead.

BIBLE-ROULETTE!

The one common denominator all humans share is failure. Mistakes have been made by every person on this planet.

I recall a time when I was a young pastor and I made what I considered to be major error in leadership. I was very concerned about how my poor judgment would affect my family and the church I served.

One morning as I was trying to begin my morning devotions in the church sanctuary, still reeling from my recent failure, I had a profound experience. Shrouded in my own manufactured gloom, I was finding it difficult to pray and to read the Bible.

I decided to just open the Word and put my finger on the first verse it landed on, hoping to find some comfort in scripture (a method called Bible-roulette, a form of study I don't recommend).

God was merciful to me in this haphazard approach of connecting with His Word. My finger fell into the book of Job, which I felt was appropriate due to my current woeful feelings.

Specifically, my finger landed on Job 32:9. Here's how it reads in the King James Version: *"Great men are not always wise: neither do the aged understand judgment."*

As I looked at this verse, obtained in my reckless Bible study method, my heart was comforted. I was able to accept the fact that I was human.

HOPE AND HEALING

The word "human" is related to the Latin word *humus*, which means earth.

As humans, we are of this earth. We are fraught with frailty and weaknesses and we all make mistakes. We are "earthy people" not divine gods.

> ❖
>
> *"Two things I know: There is a God and I am not Him."*

Someone once gave me a T-shirt I loved. Printed on the front were these words: "Two things I know: There is a God and I am not Him."

That sums it up. We are all human, and we make many missteps on life's journey. We fail in raising our kids, leading our companies, being good spouses and friends. And so often we fail God.

However, the mental concession that we all make mistakes doesn't give us permission to have a lax attitude concerning our tendency toward failure, but it gives us hope and healing when we have failed.

MOMENTS OF FAILURE

I read once of some rather humorous mistakes made by inventors. Stephen Pile wrote a book entitled *The Book of Failures* in which he documents some of the greatest goofs of history. His book chronicles moments of failure including:

Like the time back in 1978 during the fireman's strike in England. It made possible one of the greatest animal rescue attempts of all time. Valiantly, the British Army had taken over emergency firefighting. On January 14 they were called out by an elderly lady in South London to retrieve her cat. They arrived with impressive haste, very cleverly and carefully rescued the cat, and started to drive away. But the lady was so grateful she invited the squad of heroes in for tea. Driving off later with fond farewells and warm waving of arms, they ran over the cat and killed it.

The prize for the most useless weapon of all times goes to the Russians. They invented the "dog mine." The plan was to train the dogs to associate food with the undersides of tanks, in the hope that they would run hungrily beneath advancing Panzer divisions. Bombs were then strapped to the dog's backs, which endangered the dogs to the point where no insurance company would look at them. Unfortunately, the dogs associated food solely with Russian tanks. The plan was begun the first day of the Russian involvement in World War II...and abandoned on day two. The dogs with bombs on their backs forced an entire Soviet division to retreat.

Rewrite Your Story

While our mistakes may not be as dramatic as some of those recorded in Pile's book, we have certainly had our share. Our failures may not be chronicled for the entire world to read, but they have been imprinted in our own mind and live long after they were committed.

> ❖
>
> *What really matters when we fail is that we don't mentally remain in "failure land."*

Every sports figure has made errors. Even the greatest quarterbacks throw interceptions, and the best baseball hitters often go down swinging. The famed Babe Ruth was once asked what went through his mind after he struck out. "I think about hitting home runs," he answered.

What really matters when we fail is that we don't mentally remain in "failure land." We have to assert ourselves like David in Ziklag and declare, "I will not live in regret but rise up and do something about my future."

David's story had a positive ending. He recovered everything he and his men had lost as the result of the Amalekite invasion (See 1 Samuel 30:18).

How different the story would have ended if David had continued with his obsession to fight with the Philistines.

Our future also depends on how we deal with the things we feel sorry about. But remember, with God's help, we have the power to write the ending of our own story.

THE FUTILITY OF REGRET

If you are stuck in the past, you cannot adequately live in the present. Regret paralyzes and prevents us from living the best life we can in the only real time we have—which is now.

Too many people reside in what I call "non-existent time." Your past is in this category; closed to you and unavailable for alteration.

Obsession with yesterday's failures is like trying to run a marathon with a grand piano chained to your leg. If we are successfully going to complete the race set before us we must banish regret from our thinking.

Self blame can seriously diminish our energy for the current challenges at hand. It is much like leaving your car lights on while you are at the theater watching a movie. The net result is a dead battery and a car that refuses to start.

Regret drains us emotionally and we are not able to move ahead.

THE PAST IS FOREVER GONE

I love the statement made by the famous missionary and explorer David Livingston. He once remarked, "I will go anywhere as long as it is forward."

How often have we said to ourselves, "If only I could go back and do that all over again."

Regret also has an element of insanity. It is the longing to reach into the past to fix a mistake we made yesterday, last month, or last year. But it is impossible to reenter the past and change anything.

How often have we said to ourselves, "If only I could go back and do that all over again."

Well, that's impossible. The past is enshrouded with a powerful force-field that prohibits anyone from reentering it ever again. How insane it would be for you to keep going to a local department store that has gone out of business. The store is empty, the doors are locked, and the contents in the building are long gone, yet you show up day after day hoping to enter the store to shop.

Likewise, you and I cannot walk into our history.

The past is closed, but the future is wide open.

SIN AND MORAL FAILURES

Not all of our humanness is simply bad judgment on the job or mistakes on a math quiz. Some of our failures are moral violations against God's Word.

Not all of our humanness is simply bad judgment on the job or mistakes on a math quiz.

It is true that we all have sinned in some form or fashion. Our sin may have been an outburst of anger, some hurtful and cutting remark we made toward a loved one, or some lustful indulgence. According to the apostle Paul, and later addressed by Saint Augustine, each of us possesses a sinful nature that gives us a natural propensity toward iniquity. This ancient church doctrine is called "Original Sin."

Paul put it succinctly: *"For all have sinned and fall short of the glory of God"* (Romans 3:2).

The word for sin in this text is the Greek word *harmatia*—meaning to miss the mark. *Harmatia* is the term that describes an archer shooting at a target and missing it.

TOTAL HONESTY

How should we respond to our own sin? We are to confess it to the Lord. The Bible tells us, *"If we confess our sins, he is faithful and just and will forgive us our sins and purify us from all unrighteousness. If we claim we have not sinned, we make him out to be a liar and his word has no place in our lives"* (1 John 1:9-10).

The word *confess* means "to agree with." The Greek word is *homologeo*—"to say the same things as another."

Confessing your sin is not arguing with God over your actions. Neither is it debating with the Lord or trying to justify what you did. It is accepting the fact that you were solely responsible for your negative behavior and broke God's law.

The Lord's response to your honest ownership of your moral failure is to lovingly forgive you. He completely cleanses us of our impurities.

CHALK ON THE BLACKBOARD

I remember when I was in the sixth grade. My teacher, Ted Shepherd, would fill the old fashioned blackboard with dates and facts during his lectures in social studies, science, and math. There were no dry marker boards or PowerPoint presentations in those days; just the old blackboard.

After an entire day of teaching our class, the board would be smudged and marked from all the lessons. A layer of chalk dust covered most of it from being written on and erased over and over again, and when we left school in the afternoon, the blackboard would be covered with blemishes from the day's activities.

Arriving in school the next morning I was always amazed at how clean the blackboard looked. There was no white chalk dust and no left over chalk lines; the board was squeaky clean. This was because when we left school the day before, the janitors came into each room with buckets, squeegees, and sponges and wiped clean the soiled boards.

In the same way, when we confess and forsake our sins, God cleanses our heart and mind from guilt and shame, which are always the effects of our trespasses.

The Lord extends His mercy toward humble people who bring their sins before His eyes in repentance and forgiveness. Scripture makes it plain that there is always a positive reaction from God to our genuine repentance. We have this great promise: *"He who conceals his sins does not prosper, but whoever confesses and renounces them finds mercy"* (Proverbs 28:13).

A SPIRIT OF HUMILITY

There are times when it is very healthy to confess your sin to a faithful spiritual friend, Christian counselor, or church leader—as well as to God. This principle is found in James 5:16 and simply says: *"Therefore confess your sins to each other and pray for each other so that you may be healed. The prayer of a righteous man is powerful and effective."*

What is the possible benefit of sharing your shame and transgression with another human being? It is that the process of confession produces a spirit of humility within us. Where God finds humility He is at work, and where there is pride He is absent.

Scripture says in three different places that the Lord resists the proud, but He gives grace to the humble (See Proverbs 3:34; James 4:6; 1 Peter 5:5.)

If you walk in humility by confessing your sin, you open the door for the power of God to work in your life. If you continue to hide your iniquity it will remain enthroned over your will and continue to defeat you. But exposure of your sin breaks its hold over your life.

God doesn't keep us in the penalty box for our sin when we have acknowledged and confessed it to Him.

When you confess your trespasses to the Lord, your conscience will be cleansed. (See Hebrews 9:14.)

God doesn't keep us in the penalty box for our sin when we have acknowledged and confessed it to Him. Now is the time to release your guilt and begin a positive future.

Why should you remember your sin if God chooses not to? *"For as high as the heavens are above the earth, so great is his love for those who fear him; as far as the east is from the west, so far has he removed our transgressions from us. As a father has compassion on his children, so the Lord has compassion on those who fear him"* (Psalm 103:11-13).

The Bishop's Sins

Keith Miller, in his book *The Scent of Love*, tells the story of a priest who kept having visions of Jesus. This humble priest went to speak with his bishop about these continued mystical experiences. He told him of his recurring visions, but the bishop was skeptical.

The church official said to the young priest, "If Jesus ever appears to you again, ask Him what the bishop's sin was before he became a bishop."

"I will certainly ask Him," replied the priest.

A few weeks later as the bishop came to his office he saw the young priest waiting to talk with him. After calling him in, the bishop asked, "Are you here because Jesus appeared to you again?"

"Yes," the humble priest replied.

The bishop inquired, "Did you ask him what the bishop's sin was before he became a bishop?"

"Yes, I did."

With a bit of a gulp in his throat, the bishop asked, "What did He say?"

The young priest replied "Jesus said, 'I don't remember.'"

Into the River

If your sin or negative actions have hurt another

person, you may need to make things right with the individual you have harmed. It is the only way to totally let go of regret.

Most of our actions are not performed in isolation—they are linked to the lives of others. What we do affects them.

Most of our actions are not performed in isolation—they are linked to the lives of others.

I once heard the story that happened long ago of a young boy who was quite mischievous. One day he pushed the outhouse into the river that ran through the farm he lived on with his family. It tumbled down the side of the hill and into the water where it was briskly carried down stream.

Later in the day, his father confronted him. "Son did you push the outhouse into the river?"

The young boy, recalling how George Washington chopped down the cherry tree, told the truth, and was not punished, replied, "Yes father, I did push the outhouse into the river."

The irate father told his son that he would receive a whipping for what he did.

"But why?" protested the son. "When George Washington told the truth about cutting down the cherry tree his father didn't punish him."

"That is true" said the boy's dad. "But George Washington's father was not in the cherry tree when he cut it down!"

MAKING RESTITUTION

If our sin is a violation of others we need to retrace our steps—as much as humanly possible—and make amends. However, if the person we have wronged is deceased, we are not in bondage to regret. Scripture says, *"If it is possible, as far as it depends on you, live at peace with everyone"* (Romans 12:18).

This means if our actions have affected other people's resources, then we must return to them what they were denied because of what we have done. If we have besmirched their reputation, then we must do what we can to reestablish their good name. Our actions must seek to repair the damage we have caused.

❖

Our actions must seek to repair the damage we have caused.

This maybe be costly, complicated, and painful for us, but our willingness to rectify the negative effect of our behavior will be richly rewarded by the Lord.

This was the approach taken by Zaccheus, the greedy tax collector who Jesus reached out to during His ministry on earth.

Zaccheus was so radically changed by meeting Jesus, that out of gratitude and appreciation of his new life, he made a vow to abundantly give back to people he had wronged in the past.

This tax collector stood up and said, *"Look, Lord! Here and now I give half of my possessions to the poor, and if I have cheated anybody out of anything, I will pay back four times the amount"* (Luke 19:8).

Confession and repentance are the spiritual side of

dealing with our sins and mistakes, while restitution is the practical side. Once you have done all you can to make amends, kiss regret goodbye and move on.

THE POWER OF RESILIENCY

I firmly believe there is no virtue in permanent regret. It is toxic to our soul and holds us back from living the kind of future God has planned. We need to replace regret with resiliency.

In his book, *Your Attitude: Key to Success*, John Maxwell tells this story about Thomas Edison:

> *Recently I was reading a brief but stimulating biography of Thomas Edison written by his son. What an amazing character! Thanks to his genius, we enjoy the microphone, the phonograph, the incandescent light, the storage battery, talking movies and more than a thousand other inventions. But beyond all that, Edison was a man who refused to be discouraged. His contagious optimism affected all those around him.*
>
> *His son recalled a freezing December night in 1914. The unfruitful experiment on the nickel-iron-alkaline storage battery, a 10-year project, had put Edison on a financial tightrope. He was still solvent only because of profits from movie and record production.*
>
> *On that December evening the cry "fire!" echoed through the plant. Spontaneous combustion had broken out in the film room. Within minutes all the packing compounds, celluloid for*

records and film and other flammable goods were burning. Fire companies from eight surrounding towns arrived, but the heat was so intense and the water pressure so low that attempts to douse the flames were futile. Everything was being destroyed.

When he couldn't find his father the son became concerned. Was he safe? With all his assets being destroyed, would his spirit be broken? Soon he saw his father in the plant yard running toward him "Where's mom" shouted the inventor.

"Go get her, son! Tell her to hurry and bring her friends! They'll never see a fire like this again!"

Early the next morning, long before dawn, with the fire barely under control, Edison called his employees together and made an incredible announcement. "We're rebuilding!" He told one man to lease all the machine shops in the area. He told another to obtain a wrecking crane from the Erie Railroad Company. Then almost as an after thought, he added, "Oh, by the way, anybody know where we can get some money?"

LOOK TOWARD THE HORIZON

David didn't stay in the grip of regret when he lost Ziklag to a fire, and Thomas Edison didn't remain in the clutches of regret when everything went up in flames. Both of these men didn't look backward, they looked forward.

In the words of Paul, *"But one thing I do: Forgetting what is behind and straining toward what is ahead"* (Philippians 3:13).

Our thinking and our outlook are always elevated when we look toward the horizon instead of the sunset. What direction are you facing?

4

Eliminating our Distance from God

*We have escaped like a bird out of
the fowler's snare; the snare has been
broken, and we have escaped.*

— Psalm 124:7

D r. Stan Coffey of Amarillo, Texas, once told this amusing story.

> *A mailman got a new route and was trying to become familiar with what to expect each day. On one porch was a mean-looking German shepherd who looked poised to leap at any minute. As the mailman casually approached the mailbox, the dog jumped twenty feet into the air, returned to the same perch on the porch, and sat down.*

The owner walked out the door to check on the commotion. The mailman asked in amazement. Why did he do that? The owner replied, Oh, we took his chain off yesterday and he hasn't realized it yet.

SO FAR AWAY

One of the reasons we have a deflated attitude is that either we haven't yet embraced the forgiveness of Christ for our sins, or we have received His forgiveness but have not adequately reflected on the good news that we are fully forgiven.

We are still thinking and acting like we are chained to guilt and shame. As a result, we feel isolated and lonely—and this makes us think we are distant from God and from others.

Carol King used to sing a song called *So Far Away*. Those of us who are baby boomers can hear that favorite sixties tune immediately in our heads. (I grew up in that era and hate to be biased—but our generation did have the best music.)

So far away, doesn't anybody stay in one place anymore?
It would be so fine to see your face at my door.
And it doesn't help to know you're so far away.
Long ago I reached for you, and there you stood,
Holding you again could only do me good,

How I wish I could, but you're so far away.

This song is about separation and isolation—a theme that most of us can identify with. There are times when we don't feel close to others, and not even close to God. We have this prevailing sense of detachment and solitude.

THE PAIN OF SEPARATION

The young man or woman who is moving away from home to serve in the military knows this feeling of separation. All of the surroundings now look different. Everything around them has changed, and they feel a sense of not being connected to others. It is also true of the young woman who moves away from her home

There are times when we don't feel close to others, and not even close to God.

area with her husband and children. The displaced young wife is now separated from her mom who she saw every day. They talk on the phone, but it isn't the same as eating lunch together in the food court at the mall.

This feeling of separation is also real for the businessman who recently lost a working partner in the company. They had brainstormed and solved problems for over fifteen years together. Now the partner has gone to greener pastures and the left-behind associate feels a gulf between him and his former colleague.

The sense of "we are here and everyone else is way over there" is a feeling that is familiar to many—and it is often difficult for most people to process.

"WHY HAVE YOU FORSAKEN ME?"

As humans, we were made for relationships, yet sometimes these links become broken. We were once close to certain people, but now they seem so far away. This feeling of distance is not confined to people; we can also feel detached from our Creator.

David, the psalmist and King of Israel, confessed how

We were once close to certain people, but now they seem so far away.

far away God seemed to him at one point. His words are abrupt and brutally honest: *"My God, my God, why have you forsaken me? Why are you so far from saving me, so far from the words of my groaning? O my God, I cry out by day, but you do not answer, by night, and am not silent"* (Psalm 22:1-2).

David's desperation for a sense of God's reassuring presence is one most believers have experienced in their journey of faith. A feeling of separation from the Lord and from others is all too common. A sense of isolation can sap our confidence and diminish a positive attitude toward life and the future.

THE TEN LEPERS

Six months before Jesus was crucified, His itinerary had Him gradually moving toward Jerusalem for the feast of the Passover in approximately 33 A.D. Somewhere along the way, on the outskirts of an unnamed village, Jesus encountered a pitiful scene. Here's how the Bible describes what took place:

Now on his way to Jerusalem, Jesus traveled along the border between Samaria and Galilee. As he was going into a village, ten men who had leprosy met him. They stood at a distance and called out in a loud voice, "Jesus, Master, have pity on us!"

When he saw them, he said, "Go, show yourselves to the priests." And as they went, they were cleansed. One of them, when he saw he was healed, came back, praising God in a loud voice. He threw himself at Jesus' feet and thanked him —and he was a Samaritan.

Jesus asked, "Were not all ten cleansed? Where are the other nine? Was no one found to return and give praise to God except this foreigner?"

Then he said to him, "Rise and go; your faith has made you well" (Luke 17:11-19).

Social Outcasts

Scripture tells us how they cried with a loud voice—which was justified because they were a distance away from Jesus. In all probability the lepers shouted out because of the emotional pain of their desperate situation. They had serious issues to contend with, a fatal disease coupled with the fact that they were social outcasts. Their distance from Jesus was a socially imposed buffer. Leprosy was believed to be contagious so they were required to identify themselves when other people approached. Consequently, they had to keep their distance from Jesus.

They were separated from God's Son—and He was physically separated from them.

Jesus eliminated the need for separation by performing a miracle.

Every time I read this story I can visualize the scene: Jesus with His disciples were in one area, and the lepers who had banded together to try and survive were far away. Verse 12 tells us, "They stood at a distance."

Jesus, however, eliminated the need for separation by performing a miracle—which was the result of the men taking the Lord at His word.

Somewhere in the midst of their first few steps, in obeying Jesus by going to show themselves to the priests (to fulfill Leviticus 14), the men were healed.

Having recognized that he was cleansed, one of the

lepers, a Samaritan, ran back to the Lord. This time he ignored the distance rule because he was no longer a leper. He gratefully fell at Jesus' feet, enthusiastically giving thanks for his recently acquired miracle.

When Jesus reached out to this man, it not only eliminated his disease, but removed the distance he had formerly felt between himself and the Lord.

THINGS THAT MAKE US
FEEL DISTANT FROM GOD

Sometimes we feel far away from the Lord just the way the lepers did in this story. Who caused the distance? Did we create it, or did God? What are the barriers that make us feel the Lord is on one side of the river and we are on the other?

Perhaps we have spiritual leprosy caused by our own sin. We may be truly disconnected from God because of our own moral uncleanness. Maybe our distance from Him is because we know we are involved in behavior God has forbidden, but we are doing it anyway. We are consciously and willingly engaging in something that is clearly wrong. As a result, our disobedience has created a disconnect between us and the Lord.

We cannot have fellowship and intimacy with God if we are doing something the Holy Spirit is convicting us of. The Old Testament prophet Isaiah puts it succinctly: *"But your iniquities have separated you from your God; your sins have hidden his face from you, so that he will not hear"* (Isaiah 59:2).

THE CONSEQUENCES OF DISOBEDIENCE

Jill Briscoe once told of a young lady in her church that came to her and said she had lost her spiritual joy and vitality. Jill probed. "When did you loose your joy?" she inquired.

"About six months ago," the discouraged young lady responded.

"Is there something that changed in your life six months ago?" Jill asked.

"Well," said the young woman, "the only thing I can think of is that my boyfriend and I moved in together."

Jill tried to persuade the young Christian woman that there was a correlation between her lack of joy and connection with Christ because of her choice to live sexually outside of the marriage covenant (See Hebrews 13:4.)

This is such a common practice today, living together before marriage. The sheer number of people who are cohabitating is staggering. Culture seems to be dictating people's behavior in this area rather than scripture. But the true believer cannot engage in this type of wayward-ness without spiritual consequences and a feeling of being distant from the Lord.

THE MISSING GRAVY LADLE

Tim Clinton, President of the American Association of Christian Counselors and Professor at Liberty

University, one told this humorous account of a mother who went to visit her son John in college.

He was living off campus and when the mother arrived at his apartment she realized that he had a roommate—named Julie.

As they all ate dinner together, the mother was carefully watching John and Julie interact with each other. When mom had some alone time with John, she asked, "John, are you and Julie sleeping together?"

"Oh no," John protested, "Everyone has roommates these days; this is perfectly normal. Everything is on the up and up."

Some time after the mother returned home, Julie said to John, "You know, ever since your mother left, I can't find my good silver gravy ladle, the one my mom passed down to me." Julie inquired, "Do you think your mother stole my ladle?"

"This is perfectly normal. Everything is on the up and up."

John assured her, "No, I don't think so."

Julie said, "Well, your mom was here, and now the gravy ladle is missing."

John e-mailed his mother, and this is what he wrote: "Mom, Julie's gravy ladle is missing. I am not saying that you took it, and I am not saying that you didn't. All I know is that since you were here the gravy ladle is missing. Love, John."

John's mother responded: "Dear John, I am not saying that you are sleeping with Julie; I am not saying that you are not sleeping with Julie. But the fact remains that if she had been sleeping in her own bed, she would have found the gravy ladle by now. Love, Mom."

John was caught by a very discerning mother!

Knowingly engaging in activities that the Lord has clearly convicted you about through His Word will disrupt your sense of intimacy with Him.

Our feeling of distance from God can usually be traced back to the point where we chose to violate a clear command of scripture.

BREAKING THE CONNECTION

One year I purchased a basketball goal for my sons for Christmas. The next day I eagerly began to erect the new goal at the appropriate place near the driveway to our house. With posthole digger in hand I went to work to install this gift for my beloved sons.

After hours of digging, pouring cement, and putting the metal pole together, the job was almost complete. All that was needed was a little time for the cement to set up, and the fruits of my labor could begin to be enjoyed.

When I had cleaned up the construction mess, I sat down in my easy chair in the den to enjoy some television. I picked up the remote to turn on the set, but the cable was out. Every channel had that annoying fuzzy screen with the obnoxious crackling noise coming from the speakers.

I phoned some neighbors to see if they had lost cable. Their's worked just fine. Then a funny thought occurred to me. Perhaps I had severed the cable line when I put the basketball goal up.

I was in denial about that possibility—especially when my wife Karen suggested the same. I vehemently protested, "I am smarter than that."

Reluctantly I called the cable company. They arrived the next day with a gadget that looked similar to a metal detector. The repair man used the device to trace the route of the buried cable wire. The detector beeped to indicate it was on the trail of the cable. Each systematic beep indicated that the detector was following an intact wire.

> ❖
>
> *I vehemently protested, "I am smarter than that."*

When the repairman reached the front of the basketball goal, the detector beeped rapidly indicating that this was the exact spot where the wire had been severed.

I tried to keep this news from my wife, but as you can imagine my verbal dance didn't fool her when I reported the visit of the cable man.

The lesson of the story is obvious. There was a specific time and place where my actions had broken the connection.

WALKING IN OBEDIENCE

When we have lost our intimacy with the Lord, we need to reflect back: "Where was that specific place I disobeyed Him or violated His clear word to me?"

Our disobedience destroys intimacy with the Lord. John the apostle states this clearly when he says in his

81

epistle: "*If we claim to have fellowship with him yet walk in the darkness, we lie and do not live by the truth. But if we walk in the light, as he is in the light, we have fellowship with one another, and the blood of Jesus, his Son, purifies us from all sin*" (1 John 1:6-7).

Having right thinking and a healthy attitude squarely depends on our receiving inner strength from above. Without a walk of obedience we find ourselves severed and separated from our ultimate resource of strength—the Lord (See Nehemiah 8:10).

If we have sinned and walked in disobedience, we can quickly remedy the situation by submitting to His gentle conviction, turning from our sin, and embracing His best plan for our life.

WOULD HE CALL?

I am reminded of a story about a little boy who wanted to visit a friend's house several blocks away from where he lived. The young lad inquired of his dad if he could make the trip for the first time by himself. The concerned father, who deeply loved his son, was worried about his walking that far alone. But realizing his son was getting to the age where he needed to venture out, his father reluctantly agreed.

He could make the trip by himself on one condition—that the boy would call as soon as he arrived, to let the father know that he was okay. Said the father, "If you don't call me, I will come and pick you up and you'll be grounded for a whole week."

The young boy eagerly agreed, but after he safely arrived at his friend's house, he became so involved in playing and having fun that he forgot his promise. The father at home was pacing, nervously looking at his watch, thinking his son should have called by now.

Then he had an idea. He picked up the phone, called the friend's home, let the phone ring once, and then hung up.

His son heard the phone and was reminded to call his dad. After the boy phoned home to say he

"Something reminded me to call you."

was okay, he added, "Something reminded me to call you."

When God calls us to obedience, it is always because of His love and care. His dealings with us are gentle and loving as He wants us to be safe and prosperous. Anything we do that violates His Word ultimately violates us; He wishes for us to have an abundant life (See John 10:10).

What we engage in that which is divinely prohibited it jeopardizes the quality of our lives and erects a barrier to a positive attitude.

BREAKING FREE

In one sense, Jesus' story of the ten lepers is true of many at some point in our lives. The lepers were the castaways of society—the outsiders rather than the insiders. They were the untouchables, classified as unclean and defiled.

The characterization of them being unclean is noteworthy. In fact, when Jesus healed lepers, He often declared that they were now *cleansed* instead of saying that they were now healed (See Matthew 10:8; 11:5; Luke 7:22.)

Every person at one time or another has been a spiritual leper. In biblical days, lepers were excluded not only from society but from worship in the temple. Their uncleanness was a barrier between their fellow men and God.

When Jesus commanded the lepers to go show themselves to the priests, they were cleansed and healed. Why send them to the priests? This was no doubt to fulfill the Jewish law as well as to be a testimony to the religious leaders (See Matthew 8:4).

A RITUAL OF RELEASE

However, there is another reason why Jesus instructed the lepers to present themselves to the priests. It was because the Jewish ritual of cleansing the priests would administer to the lepers was highly symbolic of what Jesus came to do.

The outline of the ritual prescribed by Moses to recognize cleansed lepers is found in the Old Testament book of Leviticus chapter 14. The priest was to take two clean live birds. One was to be killed over a vase containing fresh water. The blood from the slain bird would mingle with the water in the vase. The priest then took the live bird in his hand with a piece of cedar wood, a scarlet thread, and hyssop, and dipped them all into the bloody water.

Next, the priest sprinkled this water mixed with blood on the person being cleansed seven times and pronounced that he was clean. The living bird was then released freely into the heavens above.

The cleansed person had to wait seven days, and on the eighth day three lambs were sacrificed, two males and one female. Then a small portion of the blood from the lambs was applied to the cleansed leper's ear lobe, thumb, and big toe. Next, a drop of oil was poured into his right hand and a significant amount of oil poured on his head.

CLEANSED BY THE BLOOD

What does all this mean? The sacrifice of one bird and the release of a live bird clearly point to the substitutionary death of Jesus on the cross. He died in our place so we could be set free. Jesus said it clearly: *"So if the Son sets you free, you will be free indeed"* (John 8:36).

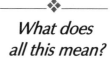

What does all this mean?

The cedar wood speaks of the cross that Jesus would die upon for man's sin in order to cleanse him. The scarlet thread symbolizes Christ's blood to protect us from God's judgment just the way Rahab the prostitute had to put a scarlet cord in her window to protect her from God's judgment that befell Jericho (See Joshua 2:18, 21).

Isaiah the prophet also said: *"'Come now, let us*

reason together,' says the Lord. 'Though your sins are like scarlet, they shall be as white as snow; though they are red as crimson, they shall be like wool'" (Isaiah 1:18).

Concerning the hyssop. It was hyssop that the children of Israel used to spread the blood of the Passover lamb on the doorpost of their homes in Egypt to protect themselves from the coming judgment (See Exodus 12:22).

The blood of the lamb applied to the different parts of the cleansed person's body speaks of the consecration of one's new life—our walk and our deeds are permanently altered by being separated to serve the Lord.

The application of oil, a symbol of the Holy Spirit, speaks of the entrance of the Holy Spirit into the person who has been forgiven and redeemed. The presence of the Holy Spirit in one's life confirms that we truly are members of the Kingdom of God.

This truth is clearly underscored in these passages:

"You, however, are controlled not by the sinful nature but by the Spirit, if the Spirit of God lives in you. And if anyone does not have the Spirit of Christ, he does not belong to Christ" (Romans 8:9).

"And you also were included in Christ when you heard the word of truth, the gospel of your salvation. Having believed, you were marked in him with a seal, the promised Holy Spirit, who is

a deposit guaranteeing our inheritance until the redemption of those who are God's possession— to the praise of his glory" (Ephesians 1:13-14).

FAULTLESS AND CLEAN

The importance of our being cleansed like lepers has to do with the major difference between us and the Lord. The Lord is holy; the Lord is impeccable in His righteousness. Our lives have been marked by sin and inconsistencies. We are, in comparison to God, unclean and unrighteous.

I once heard Chuck Swindoll tell about an interesting mishap he had while on a ministerial hospital visit one day. He somehow took a wrong turn and went through a door that led to an operating room where a surgery was in progress. The staff quickly hustled Swindoll out of the operating room because he was unsanitized. Everything in the room was scrubbed and sterile.

❖

By His death we have been set free and cleansed like the bird released in an open field.

Likewise, God and His throne are faultless and clean. For us to enter in our impure condition would offend God's holiness. But Jesus was the sacrificial bird in the Leviticus story. By His death we have been set free and cleansed like the bird released in an open field.

87

OUR DEFINING EXPERIENCE

Those who have accepted Christ and believed in His sacrificial death for their sins have been cleansed of their leprosy and are pure. In the story of the ten lepers, there was only one solution for their condition—and that was Jesus.

The thankful, healed Samaritan leper came back to Jesus and fell at His feet. No longer was he forbidden to be separated from Christ, but he could now be close to the Lord because his uncleanness was gone.

This was the most significant event that ever happened in his life and he was profoundly thankful.

Of all the marvelous events we may have encountered, a cleansed heart by Jesus is our defining experience. It becomes the basis for our gratitude.

The bedrock of a positive thought life rests on the revelation that our sins have been forgiven. On the rainiest day of our lives, our sagging emotions can be lifted because there was an incredible moment when our spiritual leprosy disappeared.

5

WHAT ARE YOU EXPECTING?

Blessed is he who expects nothing,
for he shall never be disappointed.

— ALEXANDER POPE

Two kinds of people live on this planet. Those who expect God to intervene and do marvelous things in their lives and those who don't.

The latter believe either God *can't* do anything for them or *doesn't care* to.

The Bible chronicles how the hand of God is always helping His people:

- The children of Israel crossing the Red Sea on dry ground after the Almighty separated the waters.
- The three Hebrew children surviving when cast into the furnace by an angry Nebuchadnezzar and "the fourth man" sustaining them in the fire.

- Jonah being preserved in the belly of the great fish for his preaching mission to Nineveh.

God's Word is filled with intervention stories of a caring heavenly Father reaching into the potential disasters of people and doing things for them they couldn't do for themselves.

The Bible is not a static document that just records religious ideas. It is a book marked by the supernatural.

Vance Havner once said, "Reading the Bible is like exploring an old abandoned house that hasn't had the electricity turned off; you may get a shock."

The Bible is not a static document that just records religious ideas. It is a book marked by the supernatural.

AN INDIFFERENT GOD?

The Deists, who were quite numerous in the eighteenth century in Europe and America, believed that the world was ruled by natural laws and that God no longer involved Himself in the affairs of men; He was merely a God with folded arms in the universe who watched His excellently designed wound-up clock run all on its own. His hand never reached into the daily lives of men and women to answer their prayers. He was largely indifferent to the needs of people.

Thomas Jefferson, whose talent and skill penned the words of the Declaration of Independence, held to this view. In fact he created *The Jefferson Bible* which denuded the gospels of the miracles of Jesus. What remained was the teachings and sayings of Jesus—minus the supernatural events the first century witnesses wrote about.

If you are an individual who denies the possibility of the supernatural, the Bible is going to be a treacherous minefield for you to walk through. It is replete with miracles.

I realize that negative circumstances occur; people die of diseases even though they are prayed for, and painful things happen on planet earth. There are many enigmas in this world, but I can also report with great assurance that I have seen the Lord touch people in miraculous ways. Events have been altered and lives have been forever changed

A Conduit of the Supernatural

In this chapter we will look at one miracle performed by Elisha the prophet who received his call to ministry in approximately 859 B.C. He is the featured prophet in the book of Second Kings.

If you were to subtract the miracles out of the record of his life, there would be hardly anything left to report. We don't have any teaching or preaching from Elisha; all we do have is an account of what he did. He was a prophet who operated in great power—and was a conduit of the supernatural.

This very intriguing story in the Old Testament helps us to grasp the potential that each of us has in any given situation or season of our lives. Each is unique and presents special challenges.

God is a creative God, and He uses creative ways to provide for us His children. The story you are about to read holds keys for your provision in life, but also contains a challenge that, if met, will revolutionize how much God can do in and through you.

The wife of a man from the company of the prophets cried out to Elisha, "Your servant my husband is dead, and you know that he revered the Lord. But now his creditor is coming to take my two boys as his slaves."

Elisha replied to her, "How can I help you? Tell me, what do you have in your house?"

"Your servant has nothing there at all" she said, "except a little oil."

Elisha said, "Go around and ask all your neighbors for empty jars. Don't ask for just a few. Then go inside and shut the door behind you and your sons. Pour oil into all the jars, and as each is filled, put it to one side."

She left him and afterward shut the door behind her and her sons. They brought the jars to her and she kept pouring. When all the jars were full, she said to her son, "Bring me another one." But he replied, "There is not a jar left." Then the oil stopped flowing.

She went and told the man of God, and he said, "Go, sell the oil and pay your debts. You and your sons can live on what is left" (2 Kings 4:1-7).

MORE THAN ONE CRISIS

As in most movies and great stories, this plot begins with a crisis. How will the solution be found? What form or shape will the answer to the dilemma take?

Once the answer arrives, we have resolution—and hence we have a great motion picture, or drama. Sometimes the outcome is positive while at other times negative, but the narrative must have resolution at some point.

The story we have just read had a positive ending, yet it began with not just one crisis, but multiple. It started with a sad funeral. The wife of a certain prophet is mourning the loss of her departed husband. Her heart is cloaked with sadness and sorrow,

Her heart is cloaked with sadness and sorrow.

but there are pressing pragmatic issues at hand. Economic challenges are as old as the earth and continue to this day. But with the death of her husband, this woman is left without a provider.

There is no life insurance, no government aid programs, no welfare checks, no social security, and no banks with savings accounts that can be liquidated for cash; there is not anything to fall back on. Her economic security drew its last breath when her husband drew his.

Perhaps it is a good thing at times for us to be at a place in life where there is nothing to fall back on, when the props are all gone and the support systems are exhausted. There are moments when God puts us in a place where He is our only resource—a very rich resource indeed.

THANK GOD FOR ROUGH SEAS

Notice the comforting and encouraging words of Psalm 118:9: *"It is better to take refuge in the Lord than to trust in princes."*

The writer of the book of James in the New Testament would agree: *"Listen, my dear brothers: Has not God chosen those who are poor in the eyes of the world to be rich in faith and to inherit the kingdom he promised those who love him?"* (James 2:5).

This verse seems to say that challenging circumstances are an opportunity for us to grow in our faith. Those facing huge obstacles, like the poor cited in this text, are people who develop great belief and trust to see God's intervention in their lives.

Our mindset and attitude toward problems should be one of welcome—because they give us the chance to grow.

John Maxwell once eloquently said, "A calm sea

never produces skillful sailors"

Is your personal sea a bit choppy right now? If so, you are in a marvelous position to begin essential growth and development.

THE COMPASS OF FAITH

It is also noteworthy that the protagonist in our story, who was undergoing severe challenges, was a very spiritual woman. Her husband had been a student in "the school of the prophets" begun by Elijah and continued under Elisha.

This family's deep devotion to the Lord didn't insulate them from trials, but the wife's faith became the solution to the test she was in. Her faith acted as a compass to guide her through this troublesome season.

Her faith acted as a compass to guide her through this troublesome season.

It is important to remember that our status as followers of Christ does not stop the possibility of troubles finding their way into our lives. Any teacher or preacher who promises insulation from the storms of life just because you are a believer is misleading his listeners.

PROBLEMS ARE PART OF THE PLAN

I am reminded of the parents of John the Baptist, Zechariah and Elizabeth. The Bible states that they were very godly people, yet for much of their lives they were unable to realize their greatest dream—having a child.

Was their trial related to their lack of spirituality? Absolutely not. Here is how the Bible describes the spiritual demeanor of the parents of John the Baptist: *"In the time of Herod king of Judea there was a priest named Zechariah, who belonged to the priestly division of Abijah; his wife Elizabeth was also a descendant of Aaron. **Both of them were upright in the sight of God, observing all the Lord's commandments and regulations blamelessly"** (Luke 1:5-6).*

There was no correlation between the faith of Zechariah and Elizabeth and the fact they were childless. It was not related to any spiritual deficiency, rather their circumstance was connected to the purpose of God and His desire to reveal His glory through providing a child of destiny to them late in their lives.

The timing for a child was not right for them earlier. Their years of barrenness were not a commentary on where they were spiritually; it was rather tied to a unique mission God had for them. Our struggles are connected to the Lord's purpose and plan for each of us. (See Romans 8:28.)

This being the case, our attitude toward our problems needs to evolve to the point where we are at peace with God's overarching plan.

MULTI-TASKING TRIALS

The widow had several challenges occurring at one

time. She had lost her husband; her financial well being was in peril because of a drastic loss of income due to his death. And now vicious creditors were looking to enslave her sons as compensation for her financial shortfall.

Her stress was layered and multifaceted. She was dealing with grief from the loss of her spouse and was under serious financial pressure because of the merciless debt collectors. To add to her misery, she was about to lose her sons. Her problems were suddenly compounded and the walls seemed to be closing in.

Troubles rarely arrive solo; they come in tandem with other problems.

This is precisely how so many trials are manifest in our personal world. Troubles rarely arrive solo; they come in tandem with other problems. Frequently when we are going through a difficult time, there isn't just one thing crashing, but many.

The old saying "When it rain it pours" isn't too far from reality for most people.

As you read the description of the widow's situation, you can sense the pressure mounting. Her plight reminds us of Job, how layers and layers of calamity fell upon him. His crops, livestock, and houses were destroyed or stolen, and his sons and daughters were taken from him simultaneously.

PERSEVERANCE PAID OFF

During the Civil War, Job's compelling story of

multiple difficulties became intensely personal. One day Abraham Lincoln sat hunched down in his chair behind his desk in the White House reading the Bible. Lincoln's secretary peered over his shoulder and noticed that the President was reading the book of Job.

Lincoln could surely relate to this narrative. At that time he was trying to lead the country after seven states had seceded, and other states were threatening to break away from the Union.

Talk about troubles. Lincoln was in conflict with a renegade general named George McClellan. His beloved son Willie had died of typhoid fever, and his wife Mary was mentally unstable.

Lincoln had trouble on every front. His predicament seemed impossible, yet he trudged ahead and his tenacity paid off.

We enjoy a unified country today because Lincoln refused to let go of our great republic even though his personal world was collapsing. However, his perseverance was seasoned with pain. Lincoln once candidly said, "If there is a worse place than Hell, I am in it."

In retrospect, we see that Lincoln's attitude of determination was greatly rewarded. And so will ours.

THE SOLUTIONS TO THE SHORTAGE

The story of Elisha and the widow is replete with lessons on how to adjust our thinking. The widow appealed to Elisha for help. He had been her husband's spiritual leader and, by extension, was her spiritual leader also. The scripture says she *"cried out to Elisha"* (2 Kings 4:1).

The prophet's question to her is intriguing. He asked, *"What do you have in your house?"* (verse 4) He was asking her what she had to work with.

When we enter a crisis we have a tendency to be *deficit* focused and not *asset* focused. She did have some oil, she replied, *"Your servant has nothing there at all except a little oil."*

If she had "a little oil"—at least she had something.

MORE THAN "ENOUGH"

When we are tossed on the sea of stress we have a tendency to see what we *don't* have and to overlook what we *do* have. We say to ourselves we don't have enough time or enough business, enough customers, enough education, enough friends, enough opportunities, and the list goes on.

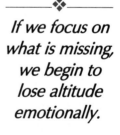

If we focus on what is missing, we begin to lose altitude emotionally.

If we focus on what is missing, we begin to lose altitude emotionally. But when we stop and take inventory of what is already ours we can begin to dream how God can cause it to multiply.

Everybody has something available to them. There is always some oil in your house, and through the Word, God has a way of putting our eyes back on what He has already given to us.

Instead of worrying over not having the ideal situation, zero in on what opportunities you currently have. When you use your energies to maximize what you possess, you will receive more. Success is realized by people who have the discipline to zoom in on opportunities, not obstacles.

This is the pattern of scripture. For example, when Moses heard God calling him to go to Egypt to liberate the ancient Jews, he said, "I am not able, I can't do it. I don't have what it takes."

> *Success is realized by people who have the discipline to zoom in on opportunities, not obstacles.*

In the biblical narrative (See Exodus 3 and 4) Moses continued to declare his incompetence (as if God needed information from Moses). Finally God stopped Moses' emotional self-doubt with a question. *"Then the Lord said to him, 'What is that in your hand?'"* (Exodus 4:2).

What God asked Moses is essentially the same question Elisha posed to the widow. Moses had a rod, and the widow had some oil—and in both cases the Lord was letting them know, "I will use what you already have to achieve victory."

ONLY A LITTLE

In your crisis, never overlook what you possess.

100

Don't obsess over your deficits—focus on your assets. This "use what you have" principle is also found in the New Testament. When Jesus fed the hungry multitudes during His ministry, He worked with a meager lunch that happened to be on hand. He didn't allow the "not enough" mentality to dominate His thinking.

When Jesus looked up and saw a great crowd coming toward him, he said to Philip, "Where shall we buy bread for these people to eat?" He asked this only to test him, for he already had in mind what he was going to do.

Philip answered him, "Eight months' wages would not buy enough bread for each one to have a bite!"

Another of his disciples, Andrew, Simon Peter's brother, spoke up, "Here is a boy with five small barley loaves and two small fish, but how far will they go among so many?"

Jesus said, "Have the people sit down." There was plenty of grass in that place, and the men sat down, about five thousand of them. Jesus then took the loaves, gave thanks, and distributed to those who were seated as much as they wanted. He did the same with the fish.

When they had all had enough to eat, he said to his disciples, "Gather the pieces that are left over. Let nothing be wasted." So they gathered them and filled twelve baskets with the pieces of the five barley loaves left over by those who had eaten (John 6:5-13).

This great miracle, which by the way is recorded in all the gospels (See also Matthew 14:13-21; Mark 6:30-

———❖———

The Lord can do more with little than we can do with much.

44: Luke 9:10-17), occurred because the attention was shifted away from what they didn't have to what they did have.

We are to take what seems insignificant and place it in the hands of God. He can do more with little than we can do with much.

DON'T BE "DEFICIT FOCUSED"

In each of these miraculous feeding accounts the disciples wanted to send the hungry people away because they were "deficit focused." They had internally declared defeat and were ready to give up. To paraphrase, Jesus told them, "Not so fast. Give me what you have and I will do something with it."

The key to this principle is that it is not what you have that matters; it is "where" what you have is located. If the little you have is in the hands of the Lord, it will always be sufficient.

"WHOSE HANDS"

Someone threaded these marvelous thoughts together:

A basketball in my hands is worth about $19. A basketball in Michael Jordan's hands is worth about 33 million. It depends on whose hands it's in...
A golf club is almost useless in my hands. A golf Club in Tiger Woods' hands means major Golf Championships. It depends on whose hands it's in...
A rod in my hands will keep away wild animals. A rod in Moses' hand will part the mighty sea. It depends on whose hands it's in...
A slingshot in my hands is a toy. A slingshot in David's hands is a mighty weapon. It depends on whose hands it's in...
Two fish and five loaves in my hands is a couple of fish sandwiches. Two fish and five loaves in Christ Jesus' hands will feed thousands. It depends on whose hands they're in.
So put your concerns, your worries, your fears, your hopes, your dreams, your families and your relationships in God's hands because it depends on whose hands they're in.

The lesson is unmistakable.
"What do you have?" Elisha asked the destitute widow.

"A little oil," she replied. God immediately turned her attention from her meager supply to His miraculous ability to multiply.

WHERE WOULD OUR THOUGHTS BE CENTERED?

When I was a young pastor, I remember seeing what the Lord could do with just a little. When we first came to the church in 1981 there were approximately 60 people and a debt of about $80,000—which seemed massive to the small congregation at that time.

In the first three months of leading the church, attendance plunged from 60 to about 25. The numbers were definitely headed in the wrong direction. It seemed people were leaving tire tread marks in the parking lot and rejecting my ministry. It was so bad that my wife and kids were considering another church! Just kidding.

The decline in numbers was in large part due to a paradigm shift I was leading the church through. As a net result of these changes we had fewer people and at first less money.

When that happened I came to the conclusion I was not going to dwell on what we *didn't* have, rather on what we *did* have. My wife Karen and I poured our lives into the people who remained. We fully invested in those who had embraced the vision God had given us. We didn't center our thoughts on finances which were dwindling, instead we were determined to be good stewards of what remained—and believed God would do something great with these resources.

The 25 faithful people have now turned into a multitude of people who worship at Bay Shore Community Church each weekend. In addition to the hundreds we minister to in person, thousands more are reached through television.

I am also thankful that the Lord has richly blessed our income as a church by faithfully providing everything we have needed as we have walked through several building programs.

> ❖
>
> *Focusing on what you have instead of what you don't have is the key to your success for the future.*

Focusing on what you have instead of what you don't have is the key to your success for the future.

RAISE YOUR SIGHTS

Elisha's counsel to the destitute widow was for her to go and ask the neighbors for assistance, for them to lend her their empty jars and containers. The prophet's instructions were clear; don't ask for a few vessels, rather ask for many. She had to be prepared for the blessing that was about to come her way—to aim high in her aspirations for provision.

Where we set our sights is so important. Often we aim far too low. This is usually because of fear, while a healthy aim is faith based.

For the poor widow it must have been humbling to

ask for help, but she did exactly what the prophet asked of her. This part of the story helps us with our thinking and attitude when it comes to traveling through the rough patches in our lives. God uses family and friends—flesh and blood people—to assist us. He also uses doctors, hospitals, counselors, pastors, spiritual leaders, and friends.

The Lord could easily have sent an angel to the widow's house with a pouch of money, but instead He used very practical means to meet her need.

ASK FOR HELP

Be careful of looking for your provision or blessing to be delivered by something hyper-mystical. God's abundance often arrives through very human means.

The widow had to ask to borrow something the Lord would use to pour out His favor on her. Asking is the key:

- If you are struggling, ask for prayer.
- If you have personal issues, ask for counsel.
- When you are about to make a major decision, ask for guidance.
- If you are lost, ask for directions.

There are men and women who hesitate to ask for anything; they want to portray a self-sufficient image. With a stiff upper lip they strive to be the picture of mental and emotional invincibility.

The underlying reason for this is pride—the antithesis of humility. But here is the view of the Almighty on this topic: *"Young men, in the same way be submissive to those who are older. All of you, clothe yourselves with humility toward one another, because, 'God opposes the proud but gives grace to the humble'"* (1 Peter 5:5).

"HUMILITY ZONES"

For the woman who had lost everything, going from door to door was a humbling exercise, but God was changing her heart, preparing her for a miracle. Always remember, the Lord performs wonders in an atmosphere of humility. "Pride zones" are miracle-free while "humility zones" are filled with the supernatural activity of God.

> ❖
>
> *The Lord performs wonders in an atmosphere of humility.*

The Lord's plan was to include her neighbors in the process. Who has God selected to help you receive your miracle? Never forget, He works through people to help move us to the place we need to be—but His greatest work takes place in our hearts as He creates a humble spirit within us.

Notice King David's advice in Psalm 51:17: *"The sacrifices of God are a broken spirit; a broken and contrite heart, O God, you will not despise."*

107

CREATING A LARGE INTERNAL CAPACITY

In the story of the widow woman, the number of vessels determined the amount of oil she would receive to pay her bills. This is an essential principle: the oil kept flowing as long as she had adequate containers. The more vessels she collected, the more oil the Lord would provide.

If she had been conservative and only visited a few houses to ask for jars, she would have only received a small quantity of oil. We are not told how many vessels she gathered, but we know that the oil didn't stop being multiplied until she ran out of vessels (See 2 Kings 4:6).

The more vessels she collected, the more oil the Lord would provide.

In this unique miracle, the capacity of the blessing was determined by the widow, not by how much oil God could supply. If she was hesitant, conservative, or doubtful, her bottom line would have been affected.

The implication in the story is that the oil would have kept flowing as long as there was a capacity to contain it. If she had gathered enough vessels to stretch around the planet, streams of oil would have continued until the very last jar was full. The number and size of the containers provided by the widow governed the magnitude of God's supply and blessing.

In this dramatic account we have a glimpse of the

limitlessness of God's grace, power, and provision. The limitation was not on the Lord's side but on hers.

PREPARE FOR MORE

The capacity in our mind and in our heart determines how much God will bless us. If you only offer the Lord one vessel, stop and ask yourself, "What am I thinking?" The Father's provision was infinite; only the containers were finite.

The lesson is obvious. Do we aim too low when we think about what the Lord wants to do for us, through us, and around us? Have we prepared a large enough capacity inside our heart for Him to fill? Have we provided the space for God to move in our family and in our business?

I recently read this account of a fisherman:

A tourist walked down a pier and watched a fisherman pull in a large fish, measure it, and throw it back. He caught a second fish, smaller this time, he measured it, and put it in his bucket. Oddly, all the large fish that he caught that measured ten inches or more he discarded. All fish smaller than ten inches he kept.

Puzzled, the curious onlooker questioned, "Pardon me, but why do you keep the little one and throw the big ones away?"

The old fellow looked up and without blinking

an eye said, "Why, because my frying pan measures only ten inches across!"

The question each of us needs to ask is, "How big is my internal frying pan?"

LIFT THE LIMITS

Do we have an expectation level that is pleasing to God?

Let me explain it this way. Perhaps your father was a shoe salesman, his father was a shoe salesman, your great grandfather was a shoe salesman, but God wants you to be a neurosurgeon.

Now there's absolutely nothing wrong with selling shoes—if this is what the Lord has ordained you to do. But if God has a call on you to save lives by being a neurosurgeon, you'd better change your plans. If you continue to have a "shoe salesman sized frying pan" in your heart and head, you may create a limitation mentally that will prevent you from reaching your life's purpose.

We determine the amount of grace and divine power that will be imparted to our hearts by God. If we fail to expand our believing capacity, we may end up with something far short of God's plan for us.

A BIGGER TENT

I love these uplifting words in Isaiah 54:1-3:

"Sing, O barren woman, you who never bore a child; burst into song, shout for joy, you who were never in labor; because more are the children of the desolate woman than of her who has a husband," says the Lord.

"Enlarge the place of your tent, stretch your tent curtains wide, do not hold back; lengthen your cords, strengthen your stakes. For you will spread out to the right and to the left; your descendants will disposses nations and settle in their desolate cities."

The prophet Isaiah was challenging the people of ancient Israel to expand the cords of their tent. In other words, there was much more that the Lord had in store for them, but they needed to adjust to get ready for this increased blessing.

❖

"Get a bigger tent to receive what I have planned for your future."

In short, the Lord was saying, "Your current tent is too small for what I desire to do through you. Get a bigger tent to receive what I have planned for your future."

It is very possible that we are currently limiting the flow of oil in our lives by restrictive thinking. Go ahead and gather more vessels for the abundance of the Lord's oil; expand your space.

111

ONLY WITH GOD'S HELP

The marvelous achievements we wish to see in our lives will not happen simply by our own efforts. We can't psyche ourselves up and produce results. Instead, begin to see that God has a great mission for each of us and He desires that we make an impact for Him.

As we align our heart with His grand vision for us, miracles beyond our comprehension begin to take place.

The psalmist expresses why it's essential to keep in step with God's will and purpose: *"If the Lord had not been on our side—let Israel say—if the Lord had not been on our side when men attacked us, when their anger flared against us, they would have swallowed us alive; the flood would have engulfed us, the torrent would have swept over us, the raging waters would have swept us away"* (Psalm 124:1-5)

David is reminding us that the Lord being on our side makes all the difference in the world.

The great vision for our lives will not be achieved by human determination alone. It will be attained by expanding our internal capacity to believe God to do bigger things in and through us. With Him as our partner, we can accomplish much more for His Kingdom than we have done in the past.

TOGETHER—ANYTHING IS POSSIBLE

Allow me to share a story from the world of sports

that appeared in a leadership publication.

One of my favorite team-play stories concerns the Chicago bulls and their then-rookie forward Stacey King. As luck would have it, on a night when King managed to score one lone point, his teammate Michael Jordan scored 69 points. When a reporter asked King after the game what he though of the evening, he replied, "I'll always remember this as the night that Michael and I combined for 70 points."

We are much like Stacey King. We have a little to contribute, but God has unbelievable resources to lift us to a level of success we have only dreamed of.

When you increase your internal capacity, you will be amazed at how far you will go and how high you will soar. Set out more vessels and watch God fill them to overflowing.

Add action to your expectations.

6

SERVANTHOOD 101

*Each of you should look not only to your
own interests, but also to the interest of others. Your
attitude should be the same as that of Christ Jesus:
Who, being in very nature God, did not consider
equality with God something to
be grasped, but made himself nothing
taking the very nature of a servant.*

– PHILIPPIANS 2:4-7

It's been said, "Happiness is like chasing a butterfly, the more you chase it the more it eludes you."

The truth is that pursuing happiness is futile. The more we try to make ourselves upbeat and joyful, the more miserable we become.

Jesus weighed in on this important point when He said, *"Whoever finds his life will lose it, and whoever loses his life for my sake will find it."* (Matthew 10:39).

Jim Elliot, the martyred missionary to the Waodani Indians in Ecuador, once observed, "He is no fool who gives what he cannot keep in order to gain what he cannot loose."

It is only through giving that we truly gain. Fullness in life is not achieved by selfishly grabbing what we can for ourselves, but in the giving of ourselves to others.

MORE THAN "SELF"

For me, servanthood was developed in my life through marriage—which has been called "the great self-eradicator." Coming in a close second in this category is having children.

> *Fullness in life is not achieved by selfishly grabbing what we can for ourselves, but in the giving of ourselves to others.*

Married at age nineteen to a beautiful young lady named Karen, I looked upon her as being the key to my happiness. She was my personal" happy-maker."

However, God had different plans and other lessons to teach me through marriage. He let me know that I was to be a giver and a self-sacrificer to this beautiful young woman.

This has been God's pattern for all marriages since the beginning. In the Garden of Eden, Adam was placed in a deep sleep and the Creator "took" from inside of him something personal—his rib.

Adam likely awoke with acute pain in his side and blood stains on his rib cage. Hiding behind the trees in the garden was his stunning new bride named Eve. In joy and excitement as he saw her beauty, he exclaimed, *"This is bone of my bones and flesh of my flesh; she shall be called woman for she was taken out of man"* (Genesis 2:23).

His relationship with Eve began with the literal giving of himself to her. The foundation of their marriage began with Adam's contribution.

WHERE WAS MOMMA?

I remember learning to give when Karen and I were first married. We were living in Pensacola, Florida, while I attended Bible College.

Karen had the flu and was suffering with nausea and a high fever. We were laying in bed one evening when she started to become nauseous. Fearing she was about to vomit, she threw the bedspread back, jumped out of the bed, and dashed toward the restroom. She fell short of her goal and expelled the body toxins on the floor in front of the bathroom door.

I could see and hear that she didn't make it to the bathroom. In my history of having the flu when I lived at home, my mother (or may we call her Momma) had always taken care of me when I was sick. If I didn't make it to the bathroom when I was nauseous, Momma would clean up the mess.

My question now was "where is Momma?"

All of a sudden I realized that I was Momma! I helped Karen back to the bed, placed a wet washcloth on her forehead and was translated into the new family janitor.

This experience was Servanthood 101 for me.

THE PRINCIPLE OF GIVING

A parallel of servanthood in scripture is Jesus washing the feet of the disciples before He went to the cross to give His life for the sins of the world. Never was there a more humble act than washing the feet of another person.

Giving, not taking, in marriage was my first major paradigm shift as a young adult. So this is what marriage was about! Earlier, I had the mistaken notion that wedded bliss was me being the recipient of Karen's extraordinary beauty and her service to me. Wrong! God's plan was for me to give to Karen.

It is through sacrifice for others that we secure our own happiness. We should not seek or try to capture it— just focus on others and in the process of giving we began to realize a deep sense of fulfillment and happiness. It's an attitude that leads to an abundant life.

MARTY PASSED THE TEST

While living in Florida during my college years, I made many friends. One was a burned out veteran from the Vietnam War named Marty Glennon. Marty was a recovering alcoholic who was in Bible College preparing for the ministry. His cool and laid back demeanor made him an appealing friend.

I was enrolled in an elective at the college for piano tuning. Having an interest in music and being an amateur musician the course was a good fit for me. The class required daily practice in tuning pianos—and the Baptist Church in Brownsville had a whole room of well-used pianos I was given permission to practice on.

One day as I came out of the church at dusk from my tuning session, I was met with a problem. My car, an awful green 1971 Ford Thunderbird, had a flat tire.

I gave a sigh and started to unlock the trunk to get the spare when Marty came buzzing down the street in his little white compact. He rolled down the window and asked what I was doing. I told him, "I have to change this flat tire and get home for dinner."

I then asked, "What are you doing?"

"Good luck with your test," I commented.

Marty replied, "I'm on my way to take a test at school?"

"Good luck with your test," I commented.

Marty pulled his car beside the curb, turned off the engine and jumped out of the car. He said, as he approached me, "I care more about your flat tire than me having to take that test."

With that, Marty rolled up his sleeves and helped me

change the tire.

Now maybe Marty wasn't ready for his test but I like to think, and knowing Marty, he was helping me because he had a huge servant's heart.

A giving lifestyle is the key to enjoying a fulfilling life.

THE MISSION

The most fulfilled person who ever lived on this earth was Jesus Himself. His life was marked by giving. He healed the sick, helped those who were discouraged, gave men and women meaning for their lives, and ultimately spilled His own blood to secure salvation for a lost and dying world.

Luke, the traveling companion of Paul, writes this about Jesus: *"How God anointed Jesus of Nazareth with the Holy Spirit and power, and how he went around doing good and healing all who were under the power of the devil, because God was with him"* (Acts 10:38).

Jesus had a mission statement for His time on earth: *"Just as the Son of Man did not come to be served, but to serve, and to give his life as a ransom for many"* (Matthew 20:28).

The life of Christ was defined by a purpose that transcended Himself. His mission was always about pleasing the Father and helping others.

If we could simplify our life's objective as Jesus did, we would enter a whole new level of joy.

THE PRESCRIPTION FOR DISCOURAGEMENT

When I first entered the ministry my father, who is also a minister, gave me this sound advice: "If you ever get discouraged and feel a little disillusioned about ministry you should leave your office at the church and go to the hospital. Start to visit sick people and pray for them and you'll find your discouragement will dissipate."

In this statement my dad told me two things about ministry: (1) it can be very discouraging, but (2) if you keep your eyes on helping others your joy will return.

I have found him to be right on both accounts. Life itself can also be disheartening: troubles on the job, problems with our health, conflicts with friends or family—there are a host of things that can weigh us down. But in the midst of it all, if you remain centered on caring for others you will make this amazing discovery: the greatest ills in life are remedied not by their elimination, but by our focus being shifted to the needs of those around us.

The greatest ills in life are remedied not by their elimination, but by our focus being shifted to the needs of those around us.

TIME FOR A DECISION

Sadly, the leaders of modern culture in film, politics,

and business tend to be self-oriented rather than others-oriented. As we watch these icons of society, we often discover that behind the glitz and glamour are lonely and empty people. They marry and divorce over and over again, trying to find the perfect person to make them happy.

Their behavior has always rotated around themselves, their popularity, and their wealth. We watch time and time again as their lives become unglued in front of the public. Their personal meltdowns show that all along, their lives were built on sand.

What a contrast from men and women who have a mission to target their energies to assist the hurting, the lonely, and those who need their help. These are the people who, in the end, find their lives brimming with peace and joy.

Long ago, Josuha issued this thought-provoking challenge: *"Choose you this day whom ye will serve"* (Joshua 24:15 KJV).

The decision you make will determine the quality of life you have. I am praying you will choose to serve God and others.

7

MENTAL WEARINESS

*The main thing is to keep
the main thing the main thing.*

— LARRY BURKETT

The greatest battle ground in the world is our mind. Our thoughts can produce incredible weariness—which is always the result of stress being poorly managed.

Pressure is an unavoidable reality. When we talk about people under stress we use phrases such as, "They are really under it right now" or "They have a lot on them."

At one time or another, each of us has felt we are carrying a heavy weight. Going through life with a huge burden is not a comfortable way to exist—nor is it the plan God has for us.

The weariness that results from tension and stress weakens our resolve and makes us want to turn our backs on what we are doing and give up. We no longer have a bounce in our step or excitement about life. Our smile fades and our hope disappears

Feeling worn out is a weight on our soul; an emotional anchor that slows us down from living to the fullest. It rears its ugly head when the pressure in our personal world becomes greater than our strength.

Here is an equation that represents what weariness may look like:

Stress + Inadequate Strength = Weariness

Too much stress plus too little strength will produce weariness every time.

If you are fatigued and worn out, you're not alone. However, there is an answer for your condition. In fact there are *three* possible solutions to controlling, even eliminating weariness.

If we understand these possibilities we can put them into practice and move toward personal freedom.

READY FOR TRANSFORMATION

The steps are simple but the implementation is difficult. Personal change is always challenging, but trying to produce change reminds me of the Kamikaze pilot on his 32nd mission; he knew what to do he was just having trouble doing it.

Usually we have to reach a point of absolute misery before we can arrive at a place where we are willing to do things differently. It is only when we are "sick and tired of being sick and tired" that we are ready to do something about our condition.

The positive side of weariness is that it usually produces a state of misery so painful that it makes us willing to undergo a transformation.

Let's look at the first step we need to take when dealing with this problem:

Step 1: Lower Your Stress Load

When we think we are required "to do it all" or feel we are obligated to perform every task people want us to, we are headed for trouble. The first step we need to make is to examine our current stress load and make some adjustments.

There are aspects of stress we *can* control which will reduce the pressure factor immensely.

A key question to ask ourselves is, "Exactly what is causing our stress and can any of those 'stressors' be eliminated?"

There are aspects of stress we can control which will reduce the pressure factor immensely.

From time to time we need to take inventory and rid ourselves of those things that are a "heavy weight" to us.

This past year, on New Year's Day, I decided to clean out my closet. I took a long hard look at my jammed-packed walk-in closet and made the decision to get rid of things I no longer wear—the clothes I haven't put on my body since the Truman administration!

I threw out the weird Hawaiian shirts that are too big for me now (I went on a diet). I put them in a trash bag bound for the Christian Shelter to be part of someone

125

else's wardrobe. And I began tossing in those out-of-style suits.

When I was finished I stood back and admired my handiwork. It was a beautiful sight to behold and I wanted to take a picture to show my friends. The closet cleaning was therapeutic for me.

When we dispose of the unnecessary clutter in our lives we begin moving toward personal freedom.

GUILT DRIVEN OBLIGATIONS

Next, we need to ask ourselves, "What am I doing just to please someone else?"

Certainly we have an obligation to please our spouse and family, but I am referring to the constant requests we receive that are all too often above and beyond the call of duty.

Guilt driven obligations should be among the first items to be discarded.

Guilt driven obligations should be among the first items to be discarded. These are the activities we are doing because we feel condemned inside if we don't.

It's as if we have an invisible person sitting on our shoulder whispering in our ear and telling us we ought to do this and we'd better do that.

Yes, we are to be servants, but other people should never set our personal agenda. Pray and ask the Lord to reveal His plan and purpose. When you find what you are passionate about, axe everything else.

YOU CAN'T PLEASE EVERYBODY

Comedian Bill Cosby once said, "I don't know the key to success, but the key to failure is trying to please everybody."

To make the point, let me share this parable:

There was an old man, a boy and a donkey. They were going to town and the boy was riding the donkey, with the old man walking alongside. As they rambled along, they passed some old women sitting in the shade. One of the women called out, "Shame on you, a great lump of a boy, riding while your old father is walking."

The man and boy decided that maybe the critics were right so they changed positions. Later they ambled by a group of mothers watching their young children play by the river. One cried out in protest, "How could you make your little boy walk in the hot sun while you ride!"

The two travelers decided that maybe they should both walk. Next they met some young men out for a stroll. "How stupid you are to walk when you have a perfectly good donkey to ride!" one yelled derisively.

So both father and son clambered onto the donkey, deciding that both should ride. They were soon settled and underway again. They next encountered some children who were on their way

127

*home from school. One girl shouted, "How mean
to put such a load on a poor little animal."*

*The old man and the boy saw no alternative.
Maybe the critics were right. They now struggled
to carry the donkey. As they crossed a bridge,
they lost their grip on the confused animal and he
fell to his death in the river.*

*And the moral, of course, is that if you try to
please everyone you will never know what to do,
it will be hard to get anywhere, you will please no
one, not even yourself, and you will probably lose
everything.*

WHO ARE YOU TRYING TO PLEASE?

Life becomes complicated and we grow frustrated
and weary when our time is spent on one big "to do" list
written by other people.

An example from scripture is helpful. Paul, the
apostle who literally penned more than half the New
Testament, struggled with constantly listening to demands of the religious leaders of his day. However he
found freedom and shows us how we can too.

Paul asked, *"Am I now trying to win the approval of
men, or of God? Or am I trying to please men? If I were
still trying to please men, I would not be a servant of
Christ"* (Galatians 1:10).

Again, let me encourage you to reduce your agenda
to these two criteria: (1) What does God want me to do

with my life? And (2) what am I truly passionate about doing?

When you discover the answers, you will find that your peace and sanity will return.

THE "DISEASE TO PLEASE"

I learned this lesson the hard way.

A few years ago I was a pastor trying to please everybody. After all, there is a little bit of a "people pleaser" in all of us. But some have what author Harriet Braiker calls the "Disease to Please" more than others.

I was highly addicted to seeing people happy and satisfied and was guilty of allowing my job description to be written by everyone in the congregation. Some thought I should be visiting any member who had a headache, others felt like I should be Dr. Phil and counsel everyone's cousin. There were those who thought I should be the ultimate administrator and, of course, everyone wanted me to deliver spell-binding sermons on Sunday morning.

> ❖
>
> *I was imprisoned by what I imagined people wanted me to do.*

The reality, however, was that much of the expectations I felt came from me and not the congregation. I was imprisoned by what I imagined people wanted me to do.

Paul the apostle had it right when he said in his epistle to the Philippians: *"This one thing I do"* (Philippians 3:13 KJV).

Personally, I could have easily changed that to, "These forty things I am trying to do."

A WAKE-UP CALL

It all came to a head one day when I was preaching an anniversary service at our church. We were celebrating over twenty years of ministry together as a congregation. I was in the pulpit waxing eloquent when all of a sudden I had trouble pronouncing some basic words. As I struggled to speak I noticed certain members of the congregation really staring at me. I didn't think what I was saying was that electrifying!

As my sermon was coming to a close, Jeff Hudson, one of our assistant pastors came up on the platform and whispered in my ear, "Karen (my wife) says for you to leave the platform; there is something wrong with you."

Well, I'd always known Karen thought something was wrong with me, but it seemed like an awkward time for her to tell me that again!

As I walked off the stage several concerned members of my family escorted me to my office. They said I was slurring my words and my face was drooping on one side. Everyone was concerned that I was having a stroke. I looked in the mirror in a restroom close to my office and saw first hand what everyone had been staring at. The right side of my face was distorted and drooping. I didn't like what I saw.

After being rushed to the emergency room at the local hospital it was determined that I was having an onset of

"Bell's palsy"—not a stroke.

I personally believe the condition was initiated by the enormous amount of stress I was under at the time. I had been over-doing it for far too long. I was also conscious of the fact that although I had not suffered a stroke, with my pressure-packed schedule, I certainly could have.

A SPIRITUAL SUPERMAN?

Due to my physical condition I was forced to slow down for awhile. For the next six weeks my face looked so unnatural that there was no way I could stand in front of a congregation to speak. During that bleak period I prayed and took long walks trying to hear the Lord's voice. One day I distinctly heard Him speak these words: "You don't have to score all of the touchdowns."

"You don't have to score all of the touchdowns."

God, knowing how much I loved football, used a metaphor that would instantly connect with me. He was saying no longer did I have to be a spiritual superman. When God called me to the ministry, He didn't issue a red cape, ordering me to leap over tall buildings.

Remembering I was but a mere man with a few spiritual gifts was the key to my future survival. I was to focus on and give my full attention to the specific things I was gifted to do. They were: public speaking and general leadership for our church. I was very blessed to have a wonderful leadership team and congregation who applauded my new approach to ministry. I empowered, supported, and encouraged others in their efforts while I stayed focused on my primary gifts.

I began to take better care of myself, lost some weight (about 40 pounds), began to exercise and started enjoying life much more. I can now look back on the Bell's palsy moment in the pulpit as a turning point in my work and ministry.

———❖———

Freedom from fatigue begins with our thinking.

Weariness can be reduced significantly with some important lifestyle adjustments. Freedom from fatigue begins with our thinking. We need to decide our priorities—what we should continue, and what we should give up. To fulfill our mission, we may need to make radical changes.

Step 2: Increase Your Strength to Compensate for Your Stress Load

The next step in removing weariness is to have increased strength.

If something is too heavy for us to carry we can either lighten the load or we can ask for help to offset the overwhelming weight. Heavy things immediately feel lighter if the load is shared.

When Karen and I built our home a number of years ago we purchased a new High Definition television. This particular model was one of the first HD sets on the market. We thought we were purchasing a cutting edge piece of technology.

Unlike the current HD television sets, this one was as big as a full-size pickup truck and seemed to weigh a million pounds.

To stay current with the times, a few years later we purchased a slimmer, more modern HD model. But what were we going to do with our old set?

I coerced my sons to help me move the "great beast" upstairs into the bonus room above our garage. It was a Herculean chore. We wondered if we would all be candidates for hernia surgery after this miserable task!

As time progressed, the bonus room became my office, but after a year I decided to move my study downstairs—and thought it would be a good idea if the old TV accompanied me there.

When I called my sons to help to move the "great beast" once again, all I heard was silence. I thought of threatening to remove them from the family inheritance, but knew that wouldn't motivate them to help old dad in this second stint at moving the monster.

Finally, I called a neighbor, an ex-Marine and his burly football player son over for some "fellowship." Because they had not seen the television before, they readily agreed to give me a hand in lowering this grand-piano of a TV to the first floor of the house. As heavy as it was, when the combined strength of three men together was synergized, it felt amazingly lighter.

The television was still the same weight it had always been, but the combined strength made all the difference.

BECOMING WEARY-FREE

Life has many heavy burdens for us to carry, yet when we combine our limited power with the One who has unlimited strength, we are on our way to being weary-free.

When we combine our limited power with the One who has unlimited strength, we are on our way to being weary-free.

Mark Batterson in his book, *In a Pit with a Lion on a Snowy Day*, has this to say concerning the Lord's ability: "To the infinite all finites are equal."

I love this statement. It is a sophisticated way of articulating that since God has unlimited strength—all challenges, big or small, are the same to Him. With just one touch, He can lift the heaviest burden off your shoulders. The amount of weight doesn't matter to the Lord because He is omnipotent—all-powerful.

Step 3: Lower your stress <u>and</u> increase your strength.

When you combine step one (reducing your stress load) with step two (increasing your strength), suddenly your ability to deal with weariness multiplies.

About seven hundred years before Jesus came to this earth, the prophet Isaiah foretold of the impending fall of the nation of Israel, but also of its restoration. His words are comforting for all who are coping with enormous pressure and stress.

Do you not know? Have you not heard? The Lord is the everlasting God, the Creator of the ends of the earth. He will not grow tired or weary, and his understanding no one can fathom.

He gives strength to the weary and increases the power of the weak. Even youths grow tired and weary, and young men stumble and fall; but those who hope in the Lord will renew their strength. They will soar on wings like eagles; they will run and not grow weary, they will walk and not be faint (Isaiah 40:28-31).

There is such a contrast between God and man in these verses:

- God is everlasting and eternal; we are not.
- He has no beginning.
- His presence and person precedes all things.
- He is the Creator; we are the created.
- God never grows tired or weary; we are subject to being fatigued.
- There is no limit to His understanding; our understanding is definitely limited.

Freedom is ours when we grasp the full implication of what Isaiah wrote in this statement. He reminds us that we are not God, yet God stands by ready to reenergize the weary.

Even young people grow tired. Working college students, during finals in the prime of their life, often feel exhausted. Young mothers running after toddlers can definitely relate to weariness. So can sleep-deprived medical interns.

INTERTWINED

The King James version of Isaiah 40:18 reads, *"They that wait upon the Lord"* will renew their strength. And in the New International Version the verse says *"Those who hope in the Lord..."*

In this context, the word *wait* or *hope* literally means to "twist together." It is the picture of two pieces of rope intertwined or twirled together to make the rope stronger.

When we rely and depend on the Lord—when we position ourselves in a place of reliance—our limited strength is supplemented and reinforced in a way that counteracts our weariness.

UNDERGIRDING THE WEIGHT

During Isaiah's lifetime, the people were in dire straits and questioned the ability of God to help them in their time of difficulty and weariness.

The rebuke of the Almighty was direct and timeless: *"Surely the arm of the Lord is not too short to save, nor his ear too dull to hear"* (Isaiah 59:1).

God's capabilities to help you are still intact. His arms can and will reach you wherever you are. He may not choose to remove all of the obstacles in your path, but rest assured, He will increase your strength.

The load you are under will no longer feel overwhelming because His arms are undergirding the weight that has been wearing you down.

Jesus is still saying," *"Come to me, all you who are weary and burdened, and I will give you rest"* (Matthew 11:28).

❖

God's capabilities to help you are still intact.

STRENGTH BEYOND OURSELVES

Freedom from fatigue is not a matter of sheer will power or determination. It is the result of being twisted together with the Unbreakable One. When your finite strength is blended with His infinite strength, your weariness will become history.

I never tire of hearing the remarkable story of Corrie ten Boom. She survived a Nazi prison camp during World War II. This woman suffered unbelievable hardship, yet her faith remained strong because her thinking was rooted in God's Word.

Corrie told the story of a woodpecker who was busily pecking on a hardwood tree in the forest.

137

Suddenly a bolt of lightning hit the top of the tree the woodpecker had been pecking on.

The tree split in half from the power of the lightning strike—and the proud woodpecker flew away squawking, "Look what I did, look what I did!"

When it finally dawns on us that our strength is derived from the Lord, we are greatly humbled. No longer can we revel in our arrogance that we are secure in our own strength. We realize that our power and victory comes from the One who never grows weary.

What a time of celebration it is when we find strength beyond ourselves.

8

THINKING TOO MUCH ABOUT TOMORROW

Yesterday is history. Tomorrow is a mystery.
Today is a gift. That is why it is called the present.
— FROM THE MOVIE, KUNG FU PANDA

I may be mistaken, but it seems that some people have a "worry" gene.

Maybe worrying isn't genetic, but we are all conditioned by the people we grow up with to have at least some anxiety.

My maternal grandmother, whom I spent a lot of time with when I was a child, was a professional worrier. She had a fear of storms, the IRS, plagues, house fires, crop failure, tornadoes, presidents canceling social security, and someone having an accident on her farm and suing her.

She excessively worried over her family drowning when they went to a lake or ocean to swim. When we would pick her up and take her to town to go grocery shopping she would cautiously come out of her farm house clutching her black patented pocketbook. She would be hunched over as she took out her keys and carefully locked her front door. Then she would look through the window to make sure she had turned the stove off—fearing she had left the oven on and would burn her house down.

After peering through the window for what seemed like an eternity, she would slowly turn around and head down the steps. Half way down, she would stop. Then she would turn around and head back up the steps to look through her door window one more time to convince herself the stove was indeed turned off.

_____❖_____

She was a bundle of nerves.

She performed this ritual every time we picked her up. Of course, it was accompanied by my mother honking the car horn and me sighing with impatience in the back seat.

I deeply loved my grandmother but she was a bundle of nerves, constantly prone to anxiety. She had a tendency to believe bad things were always about to happen.

From her conversations with me as a child I gathered that her father, my great grandfather was a professional worrier as well. For instance she said he shared her terror of storms.

ONE MORE LOOK

When I went to college I discovered I had assimilated some of my grandmother's worrying tendencies. After a class was finished I would look carefully under my desk to make sure I had gathered up all of my books. Then, as I was about to walk out of the classroom, I'd have this terrible fear that I had left a text book under my desk. So back I would go to look one more time.

One day it occurred to me that I was replicating my grandmother's ritual of looking in the window to make sure the stove was off. Now there's no crime in being thorough and careful, but this illustrates how some have a tendency toward anxiety and worry more than others. No one knows for sure whether it is a result of our temperament or our environment.

IS IT WORTH THE WORRY?

In her book, *A Marriage Made in Heaven: or Too Tired For an Affair*, the late Erma Bombeck admits she was a worrier:

> *I've always worried a lot and frankly, I'm good at it. I worry about introducing people and going blank when I get to my mother. I worry*

about the shortage of ball bearings; a snake coming up through the kitchen drain. I worry about the world ending at midnight and getting stuck with three hours on a twenty-four hour cold capsule. I worry about getting into the Guinness World Book of Records under "Pregnancy: Oldest recorded birth."

I worry what the dog thinks when he see me coming out of the shower; that one of my children will marry an Eskimo who will set me adrift on an iceberg when I can no longer feed myself. I worry about salesladies following me into the fitting room, oil slicks, and Carol Channing going bald. I worry about scientist discovering someday that lettuce has been fattening all along."

What is ironic, if not down right funny, is that people who tend toward worry usually marry non-worriers. This creates tension because the worrying spouse is annoyed that the non-worrying spouse never worries—which makes the worrying spouse worry more!

If you are anxiety-driven, what follows is especially for you.

HOW TO CATCH A FLY

Have you ever had an annoying house fly you were trying to swat or catch? Flies can be very allusive. However, one shouldn't waste time over the great mystery of catching flies because a really smart person has conducted a study on this perplexing question; there are studies on everything these days—including this topic.

Here is the conclusion of the art of fly catching:

Do you know the best way to swat a fly? According to the scientific journal, Nature, the best way is to take a piece of tissue paper in each hand. Approach the fly from the left and right at the same time, keeping the hands equidistant from the fly and moving to and fro slightly. Then with both hands simultaneously pounce.

The advice is soundly grounded in "fly-neuroscience." Dr. Edward Gray of England's University College, London, writes: "The fly cannot cope with this situation, since its central nervous system circuitry is geared to avoid approaching movement in only one part of its visual field at a time.

Two simultaneously approaching threats render the fly immobile, for its central nervous system now cannot compute at which angle to take off.

According to this research, flies become vulnerable when they try to concentrate on too many things at once. They are fleet winged and illusive when they have a single focus. When flies try to see more than one thing at a time, they are immobilized and ultimately doomed. In this aspect humans are like flies. When we try to focus on yesterday, today and tomorrow we experience emotional overload and can't function properly.

LOOK AT THE BIRDS

Man was designed to live one day at a time. When you and I center our thoughts on the present we soar; if

Man was designed to live one day at a time.

we add obsessive thoughts concerning what could happen tomorrow we quickly crash.

Two thousand years ago Jesus stood on the side of a mountain and talked on the topic of being too worried. His words are timeless:

> *Therefore I tell you, do not worry about your life, what you will eat or drink; or about your body, what you will wear. Is not life more important than food, and the body more important than clothes? Look at the birds of the air; they do not sow or reap or store away in barns, and yet your heavenly Father feeds them. Are you not much more valuable than they? Who of you by worrying can add a single hour to his life?*
>
> *And why do you worry about clothes? See how the lilies of the field grow. They do not labor or spin. Yet I tell you that not even Solomon in all his*

144

splendor was dressed like one of these. If that is how God clothes the grass of the field, which is here today and tomorrow is thrown into the fire, will he not much more clothe you, O you of little faith?

So do not worry, saying, "What shall we eat?" or "What shall we drink?" or "What shall we wear?" For the pagans run after all these things, and your heavenly Father knows that you need them.

But seek first his kingdom and his righteousness, and all these things will be given to you as well. Therefore do not worry about tomorrow, for tomorrow will worry about itself. Each day has enough trouble of its own (Matthew 6:25-34).

A NEW VIEW OF THE FUTURE

Evidently anxiety and worry are not new to the human race. The people Jesus was speaking to lived in more challenging times than we do. Think about it. They had no health insurance (and no hospitals for that matter), no unemployment benefits, no social security, no retirement plans, mutual funds, or stock options. In fact, these ancient men and women didn't even have refrigerators or freezers to preserve their roast for Sunday's dinner!

Everything in their world depended on the weather and the availability of food. "Not surviving" was a constant threat. These people worried over the basics of life.

Ironically, we worry as much as they did, although our support systems are much more thorough and sophisticated. We have amazing systems of finances, health, education, and agriculture. Instead of being concerned about not having enough to eat, most Americans eat far too much!

We click on the TV remote and there is another diet commercial with a former obese celebrity who has lost weight—beckoning us to their particular plan. We desperately need this weight-loss program because we have gorged—and now have the gut to prove it!

Yet we worry as the ancients did—perhaps even more. However, the people in Bible times had one advantage over us: ignorance of world events.

Thanks to the Internet and television, we are privy to all the daily bad news taking place around the planet. In one moment we can be aware of a massive fire in Australia, a tsunami in Sir Lanka, or pirates hijacking a cargo ship off the coast of Somalia.

This makes the words of Jesus more important than ever. The obsession with what will happen tomorrow has always been a problem for mankind. But the Lord challenges us to adopt His view of the future. He tells us not to worry, but to trust our heavenly Father for all our daily needs.

The advice of God's Son on this matter is so simple and basic that we are tempted to dismiss it. The word "worry" Jesus uses is *merimnao*—meaning to be drawn in two different directions or to divide the mind.

FORGET THE HYPOTHETICALS

Like the fly analogy, if we try to keep our eyes on the present and the future simultaneously, our mind is divided and we are stressed.

To be "today focused" instead of "tomorrow focused" is the key to peace and abundant life. When we fast- forward ahead in our minds and begin to deal with possible hypothetical outcomes, our body—not to mention our emotions—is filled with stress.

The hypotheticals are: What if this happens?" or "What if this doesn't happen?"

❖

"What if this doesn't happen?"

If you divide your mind between *now* and *then*, you will be trapped in a cage called worry.

When you are watching a movie on your DVD player you can skip to future scenes. Mentally, we often push the same buttons to think about what could happen tomorrow. But we can never have a satisfied life if we are living in non-existent time. God is always with us in the "now" rather than the "not yet."

"GIVE US THIS DAY"

God gives us grace and ability to handle one day at a time. If we live in the present moment, we feel His strength, but when we lasso tomorrow and pull it into today we don't have sufficient strength. We are not made to shoulder two days—only one. It has always been God's plan and design.

This doesn't mean we shouldn't prepare for tomorrow in practical ways, but we cannot worry over the future if we expect to have a positive day. It violates God's principles.

In the Lord's Prayer, Jesus told us to pray these words: *"Give us this day our daily bread"* (Matthew 6:11).

He is not asking us to pray for next month's provisions, but for today's.

"WHAT IS IT?"

In the Old Testament, when the children of Israel became hungry as they were trekking across the desert, God supplied manna from heaven for them. The word *manna* literally means "what is it?"

When they saw this food on the ground it was unlike anything they had ever seen before. I can see them looking at each other, asking, "What is it?"

This was God graciously supplying what they needed for that particular day. But there was one stipulation:

> *Then Moses said to them, "No one is to keep*
> *any of it until morning." However, some of them*
> *paid no attention to Moses; they kept part of it*

148

*until morning, but it was full of maggots and
began to smell. So Moses was angry with them.
Each morning everyone gathered as much as he
needed, and when the sun grew hot, it melted
away* (Exodus 16:19-21).

The instructions were clear. God would provide them
with bread for a day—which when eaten would sustain
and give them energy and strength for the next twenty-
four hours.

Let's face it. We feel weary and
worn out when we place the
concerns of tomorrow on our

*"This is the day the
Lord has made."*

shoulders. The reason we feel overloaded is because we
have not yet received power to withstand the pressures of
future days. But when we redirect our thoughts on the
day in which we are currently living, we will feel and
realize God's inherent strength for the "now."

The psalmist understood this principle: *"This is the
day the Lord has made; let us rejoice and be glad in it"*
(Psalm 118:24).

PREPARE FOR TOMORROW

People who think saying "don't worry" is a simplistic
formula for living tend to forget that a non-worrying
lifestyle doesn't prohibit planning. God is not against
responsibility; in fact He demands it: *"If a man will not
work, he shall not eat"* (2 Thessalonians 3:10).

Jesus cited the birds in His teaching on worry. God takes care of the them, but they are not passive—the early bird *does* get the worm!

The Almighty places opportunities around birds for their provision, and they take advantage of them. But for you and me, being free from worry doesn't give us an excuse for not saving money or investing for future needs.

In the Old Testament, when a famine was on the way, Joseph stored up grain on behalf of the Israelites and Egyptians. He prudently prepared for the challenges of the future: *"Joseph collected all the food produced in those seven years of abundance in Egypt and stored it in the cities. In each city he put the food grown in the fields surrounding it. Joseph stored up huge quantities of grain, like the sand of the sea; it was so much that he stopped keeping records because it was beyond measure"* (Genesis 41:48-49).

A non-worrisome life doesn't cancel wise planning for tomorrow.

No Excuses

Obviously, students shouldn't take Jesus' words concerning worry as an excuse to neglect their homework or study sessions for exams. They should prepare and pray. As someone commented regarding the school prayer debate, "As long as there are math tests there will always be prayer in schools!"

We are to be diligent. The problem, however, arises when we have been responsible, yet we continue to be fearful and worry over what tomorrow holds.

A person who can't mentally and emotionally let go after they have done all they can is like someone driving their car home and leaving the engine running all night while they lay fast asleep in their bed.

Let me encourage you to do everything you can and let God do the rest. The Lord is much better at doing His part than you are at doing yours.

The Lord is much better at doing His part than you are at doing yours.

Noah was obedient in building the ark. Then he let in the animals, entered the vessel with his family, and sat down. It was God who sent the rain and consequent flood.

If worriers had built the ark in the desert, they would have brought out a garden hose and tried to get the boat to float! How foolish. You must be responsible; do everything you can, then sit down and leave the rest in God's capable hands.

THE INSANITY OF WORRY

Jesus reminds us that worrying is a non-productive activity. If you become upset over being too short, it won't make you taller. Or if you worry that you don't have enough time for your activities, the clock won't change. Remember the question Jesus asked: *"Who of you by worrying can add a single hour to his life?"* (Matthew 6:27).

Perhaps the number one reason we shouldn't worry is because it doesn't work! Anxious thinking has no power whatsoever to alter our future.

Worry is like spending twelve hours painting the interior of a house with a brand new—but dry—paintbrush. Regardless of how skillful your painting techniques, the color of the walls has not changed one iota, because there is no paint on the brush.

It's time to give up fear and uncertainty because it is always a useless mental exercise. Worry usually explores possible experiences that rarely, if ever, occur.

As Mark Twain humorously observed, "I have seen a lot of trouble in my time that never happened."

RUNNING FROM NOTHING

James Thurber, a cartoonist, journalist, and author in the early 1900s wrote a fascinating short story called "The Day the Dam Broke." It's about Columbus, Ohio—a small community at the time—that was terrorized one day in 1913 because everyone thought the local dam had burst and would soon flood the town.

It all began when a person started running through Columbus without saying a word. Everyone assumed that the dam had given way. After fleeing great distances the citizens finally had to admit they were running from nothing. Sheepishly, they snuck back in town, minimizing how far they had fled.

The residents of Columbus were running from an imaginary flood!

What made-up disasters are we escaping from?

THE END OF ANXIETY

Conquering mental anguish is not easy. Beating fear is a constant battle, but giving into the winds of worry will always lower the quality of our lives. In the words of the British evangelist George Muller, "The beginning of anxiety is the end of faith. The beginning of true faith is the end of anxiety."

It is my hope that from today forward you will carefully and prayerfully examine your thought life. Take a moment each morning and ask yourself, "What am I thinking?"

Stop worrying and start living!

EPILOGUE

It was a cold January 2009 afternoon at LaGuardia airport in New York City. Chesley B. (Sully) Sullenberger was settled in his pilot's seat to begin another routine flight to Charlotte, North Carolina— or so he thought.

Flight 1549 was destined to become one of the most infamous flights in recent history. The plane Sully was captain of was a magnificent eighty-ton A-320 airbus. As the excellently engineered and designed aircraft taxied toward it's designated runway around 3:20 P.M., it finally was positioned for takeoff.

At precisely 3:26 P.M. the aircraft speeded down the runway and was airborne. In less than a minute Sully radioed back to the control tower that the plane was in serious trouble. There had been, according to Sully, a "double bird strike."

He requested permission to return to LaGuardia for an emergency landing. The response was swift. He would not be able to land there but was to proceed to another nearby airport at Teterboro, New Jersey.

Sully's aircraft, with 155 passengers, including him, banked over the Bronx and hoped to make their destination to New Jersey safely. It became immediately obvious that the plane had lost the capability to reach that airport. With limited options, Sulley decided to align his large aircraft with the infamous Hudson River.

"BRACE FOR IMPACT"

The pilot, who had extensive training in psychology, aircraft design, and experience with gliders, lowered the plane toward the 36-degree frigid waters of the Hudson. His last words to the passengers were, "Brace for impact we are going down."

With heads lowered in their laps a hundred and fifty four people prayed fervently. The aircraft safely landed in the river with no loss of life. New York Governor David Patterson called it "The miracle on the Hudson."

An astonished nation watched as these inspiring events unfolded on national television. Shivering passengers wrapped in towels and blankets were ferried safely to the shore. Most of their luggage was probably lost forever but their lives were saved by their prayers and the skill of an accomplished and quick-thinking pilot.

What is amazing to me is that this eighty-ton aircraft was brought down by birds. Sophisticated and magnificent engines were paralyzed and rendered inoperative by mere birds.

CLIMB HIGHER AND HIGHER

Our thoughts are similar to those seemingly harmless birds that downed flight 1549. What we allow to enter our minds will always determine our personal altitude. Every morning when we get out of bed we choose our thoughts. There are plenty of negative concepts and ideas we can ingest, but to do so will always bring us down. The only way we can climb higher and higher is to avoid destructive, damaging thoughts.

God sees you soaring, not sinking, flying, not falling. His desire is for you to have the mind of Christ as you prepare for an eternity with Him.

Acknowledgments

I wish to thank my son, Joel, who administrated much of this publishing process for me. His passion for excellence to do all things well is reflected in this book.

Thanks to Joel and Andy for the great cover design.

Thanks to Cathy Hudson, my administrative secretary, who worked on a million details, not only for this book but for our ministry in general.

Thanks to Rhonda Sharman for her careful editing of the original manuscript.

Thanks to John McTernan, the Financial Chairman of Bay Shore Community Church and a loyal ministry partner, for his support of this book as well as the Board of Directors of BSCC.

Thanks to the wonderful people of Bay Shore Community Church who faithfully attend each week to worship God and to embrace my teaching and preaching.

Thanks to my mom and dad, Roland and Mary Ann Tice, who have faithfully served the Lord in front of our family and our community for decades and also my loving and supportive in-laws, Elmer and Jean Moore.

Thanks to my honorable sons, Tim and Joel, and their beautiful wives, Gillie and Stacy, who bring immeasurable joy and fulfillment to my heart every day.

FOR ADDITIONAL MEDIA RESOURCES OR
TO SCHEDULE THE AUTHOR FOR SPEAKING EVENTS,
CONTACT:

DANNY TICE
BAY SHORE COMMUNITY CHURCH
36759 MILLSBORO HIGHWAY
MILLSBORO, DELAWARE 19966

PHONE: 302-238-7370
INTERNET: www.bayshorecc.org
EMAIL: danny@bayshorecc.org